Financial Discipleship
... investing in eternity

By Peter J. Briscoe

Copyright Peter J. Briscoe

ISBN: 9789083031774

June 2020

All rights reserved

Published by Compass – finances God's way

European office: Zielhorsterweg 71, 3881 ZX Amersfoort, The Netherlands

www.compass1.eu

The Compass - *finances God's way*
Vision, Mission & Values

Our Vision

To see everyone, everywhere faithfully living by God's financial principles in every area of their lives.

Our Mission

Equipping people worldwide to faithfully apply God's financial principles so they may know Christ more intimately, be free to serve Him and help fund the Great Commission.

Core Values

Bible-Based

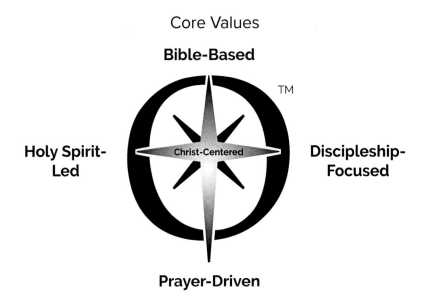

Holy Spirit-Led

Christ-Centered

Discipleship-Focused

Prayer-Driven

Table of Contents

Foreword

God wins. As Christians, we believe that to the depths of our soul.

When I was a kid, we bought off-brand everything – food, clothes, appliances, toys, you name it. My mom grew up relatively poor, and although we were the typical middle-class family in America, what she learned growing up influenced how she viewed money. It equipped her, in fact, to recognize tradeoffs and make smart choices; spending less in certain areas allowed for spending in other areas. My parents' discipline with money allowed us to take vacations every year, which resulted in some of our best memories as a family, both then and still today.

Throughout my life, God has blessed me with mentors who have reinforced the same basic principles for handling money and life: have a plan, follow a process, spend less than you make, give to get, lead by serving, and empower others to do the same. And along with these, control what you can and be ready to adjust, understanding that sometimes the unexpected happens; that's life.

My mentors modeled these principles and were passionate about their method. It was as if they'd discovered this perfect blueprint on how to successfully master money and life. All the while, they were also "teaching me how to fish" and the idea of "paying it forward." Instilling these principles in me was a big deal to them. I wonder sometimes, could mentoring be a fancy term for discipling?

When I met Howard Dayton, Founder and Chairman of Compass – finances God's way, in 2016, and later Peter Briscoe, I was struck by how interconnected the concepts of Christianity, discipleship, and money were in their lives. They modeled humility in Christ, led as Christian disciples and teachers, and were applying God's principles on finances in visible and meaningful ways. They were authentic yet sophisticated, projecting that rare combination of confidence and conviction that undoubtedly came from the Holy Spirit, along with their extensive backgrounds in business and ministry. They had the same perfect blueprint, but with an added twist: their objective was to manage money God's way as a means to get closer to Christ and be free to serve Him. It was a model built for eternal impact.

I engaged, and they unleashed Scripture on me – from strategy to tactics, from the upside to the downside, from the commands to the strong suggestions, from the here and now (earthly perspective) to the later and forever (eternal perspective) – everything the Bible said about money. Their teaching transformed me, permanently. So much so that the Lord led me out of the business world to serve with Compass as their Global CEO. What were Howard and Peter doing? The same thing they've done for 40-plus years: being financial disciples.

Financial discipleship is us doing our part to put God in the best position to win. He doesn't need our help, certainly, but He does give us a clear and important role to play. Understanding and activating our role as financial disciples within God's plan for the world is a critical component of being a complete Christian.

Money intersects nearly every area of our life. Unfortunately, relating God's formula for managing money and possessions is seldom talked about in churches, marriages, businesses, or the home. Why is that? Doesn't God have anything to say about money? And if yes, what do we do about it?

The reality is, God has a lot to say about money. He references the subject 2,350 times in the Bible. That's more than double what He says about faith and love combined! Additionally, nearly fifteen percent of everything Jesus said, and over forty percent of His parables, used money as a subject to communicate a Kingdom perspective. So it's a huge topic for God! Fortunately, He gives us clear instructions, big goals and expectations. And God-sized eternal benefits when we get it right. Similar to Peter and the entire Compass team, I've also become passionate about, maybe even obsessed with, the idea of financial discipleship as the next big frontier for us to pursue as a global Christian community.

In this book, Peter elevates the discussion on financial discipleship – what it is, why it's important, and how it fits into the Master's plan. He paints the picture of the role financial disciples can and do play on earth and in the Kingdom. He navigates through the strategy and eternal benefits of living the life of a financial disciple. He helps us to internalize the historical context of these biblical concepts on money and apply them to our lives in practical ways. Finally, he punctuates the importance of financial disciples embracing their responsibility to raise up other financial disciples, paying it forward in the process and helping to both fund and fulfill the Great Commission. This is a must read! I recommend this book to anyone who's searching for wisdom on what God says about money and how to put it to good use for the glory of God through all of eternity.

Financial discipleship is a lifestyle and a choice. It's not a journey with a defined destination, per se. Rather, it's an iterative, circular, lifelong progression that's different for everyone. The goals are relatively straightforward: to increase in awareness, faithfulness, and obedience. Progress on the goals brings the objective into focus: humility in Christ through the Holy Spirit, which produces lasting fruit that multiplies the Kingdom. Once we're living fully by the Sprit and producing lasting fruit, we're transformed, becoming disciples who are in the best position to optimize God's purpose for our lives: to glorify Him in every area of our life, especially the area where we so often fall short – our finances.

The goals, objectives, and outcomes Peter encourages us to pursue throughout the book lead to some all-important questions. In the end, what story will your money tell? Are you investing in eternity? What if you could change the economics of the world for the Kingdom and help others come closer to Christ in the process? When we implement the model and concepts outlined in this book, God wins and we grow closer to Christ as a result of our financial faithfulness. Praise and glory be to God!

Brandon Sieben
Global CEO, Compass – finances God's Way
Iowa City, Iowa, USA

Every Nation

"A financial disciple has a desire, to see every follower of Christ in every nation faithfully living by God's financial principles in every area of their lives, both personally and in work, family, and community."

About the Author

Peter Briscoe, an Englishman born in 1950, studied Industrial Chemistry and Management at Loughborough University of Technology. He moved to The Netherlands in 1974 and was asked by his company to set up a subsidiary in Holland, selling chemical specialties to the aerospace and food-processing industries. From 1986 to 1990, Peter was Executive Director of CBMC, Christian Businessmen's Committees, in Holland. CBMC is dedicated to making disciples among business and professional people.

In 1990, Peter set up Synthesys, a consulting company specializing in chemical product development. When the Berlin Wall collapsed in 1990, Peter developed Europartners, a movement dedicated to reaching and discipling European business and professional leaders for Christ.

From 2002, Peter took an assignment as Managing Director of HE Space Operations, serving the European Space institutions, specializing in providing professional services for spaceflight activities.

From 2008, Peter retired from business to develop a movement of financial discipleship in Europe that is now active in over 20 nations.

At home, Peter is Chair of the Church board of the Baptist Church of Leiden. He is married to his Dutch wife, Didie, since 1972. They are blessed with three daughters and six grandchildren.

—

INTRODUCTION

—

My journey of financial discipleship

My financial journey started as a fifteen-year-old when my father lost his job. This was very traumatic for the family. We had to uproot and leave home, moving up north to live with my aunt. All I could take with me was my dog and what I could carry. I lost things that were quite important to me, like a collection of football memorabilia, my bike, a model train set, and more. I learned from that experience that ownership is temporary. Things can be taken away from you very quickly.

A year or so later, my father was ordering things from mail order companies, nice things for his family, out of a good heart. He wanted to maintain the kind of lifestyle he was used to, but he and my mom had difficulty making the payments. I remember lying in bed one evening, listening to them argue in the next room. I learned from this that debt can be toxic. It can put enormous stress on relationships. It can even take over your whole life. I vowed never to take out a loan, and with the exception of a mortgage, I have kept the vow.

My first introduction to the concept of discipleship was as a student at university. I was introduced to some fellow students who befriended me and invited me to join a group to study the Bible and learn about following Jesus. I had been attending church since I was fifteen, having come to Christ through a youth movement. However, I had little understanding of the Bible and who God really was.

Robb Powrie-Smith led a student movement called The Navigators at my college, Loughborough University of Technology. His home was open to students who came in for coffee and a chat about Christian life. He helped me to understand the Bible, teaching me to study and even memorize portions that would enrich my soul and help me to make decisions beneficial to my life.

My friends from The Navigators helped me navigate the moral minefields of the sixties and early seventies and to become a disciple, a fully devoted follower of Jesus.

My wife and I participated in a large European conference on disciple-making in Essen, Germany in 1978, at which we were challenged to respond to Jesus' assignment to *"go and make disciples of all nations . . ."* We made that commitment together. I remember the speaker, the Navigators' International leader, Doug Sparks, challenging us, "This is just the start of a lifelong journey. The first thing to happen will be that you will be put into a training camp to learn about following Jesus through life – the hard way!"

We first had to learn about following Christ in the midst of marriage problems. I was hotly pursuing my career and ambition to become the CEO of a chemical business by the time I was thirty.

I achieved this, managing a Dutch chemical company during the serious oil crisis of 1980. We had difficulties getting raw materials for our products. Labor unrest added to the difficulty of doing business, and I suffered from quite a lot of stress. I remember sitting in church one Sunday morning and all I could think about was how to pay the bills the next day. I was a Christian on Sunday, but on Monday I was somebody else – not a good situation.

Reaching my ambitions came at a price. With all the travel and long work hours, my relationship with my wife and three small children deteriorated badly. My health suffered, and I ended up in the hospital. Unable to integrate my faith into my daily life, my relationship with God hung by a thread.

Some Christian businesspeople invited me to a Monday morning seven o'clock prayer and Bible study meeting. There I met disciples who were serious about following Jesus in their business and family lives. They helped me sort my life out and get back on track following Jesus at home and in my business and church. They were disciple makers!

I wanted to out find how I could apply my Christian faith to my daily life, how to manage a business, and how to handle money. I found some biblical teaching from the founder of Compass, Howard Dayton, who together with Larry Burkett was a pioneer in this field. I traveled to the United States to participate in the workshop "Business by the Book." The lessons learned changed my business life completely. As my wife and I translated the Compass course "Navigating Finances God's Way" into Dutch, we gained a new perspective on managing our personal finances.

I began teaching these courses and have now sown the seeds of biblical financial principles in more than fifty nations over the past thirty-five years. Through applying and teaching these truths about doing business and managing money, I have found that the goal is not merely to become a better businessman or to manage money better. That certainly happens, but it's a by-product of becoming a follower of Jesus, growing in intimacy with Him, being set free to serve, and to grow in generosity.

I looked in all these nations for "F.A.T." men and women, people who were faithful, available, and teachable. With these I have helped to set up national organizations in over fifty nations in Europe and Africa to help others follow Jesus in business and with their finances.

I was called out of active business twice to serve full time in this ministry of disciple-making around the world. First, I left my assignment as the CEO of the chemical company, and later as the CEO of a business specializing in human spaceflight – both times to start movements to disciple people, especially in the areas of business and finance. I founded and served for twelve years as president of Europartners, a Europe-wide movement of Christian business and professional people, helping others find and follow Christ to become disciples in business. I spent some years as International vice-president of Crown Financial Ministries, followed by serving as European regional director for Compass - finances God's way, helping to make financial disciples.

So, what's a financial disciple?

A financial disciple has a desire, to see every follower of Christ in every nation faithfully living by God's financial principles in every area of their lives, both personally and in work, family, and community. Just imagine a world with every business fair and honest, its people living faithfully and working by God's financial principles. I believe prosperity and well-being would be the norm for all employees and customers.

Just imagine a family living faithfully by God's financial principles: no arguments in marriage, kids brought up to know how to manage their money wisely, a prosperous future for the whole family. Our churches would be fully funded by generous financial disciples and people would freely volunteer for the work of the Church. Free from the burden of debt, people would be free to give their time and talents to serve their neighbors.

Financial disciples help others follow Jesus with their money and possessions so they can experience the activity of Christ Himself in their daily lives.

As I write this book, I am approaching seventy years of age and have been consciously following Jesus since I was sixteen. The journey of discipleship has been one of ups and downs, traveling from hills through valleys to mountains and down again! However, the upward call of Jesus is still strong.

I thoroughly believe that finances are at the cutting edge of discipleship. The way we use our money is a direct reflection of our priorities. I remember being told, by a wise, old mentor, "Show me your bank statement, and I will show you what you live for – what your priorities are. If you say that God is the most important thing in your life and this is not reflected in your bank statement, you are fooling yourself."

He based this on Jesus' words, *"Where your treasure is, there your heart will be also"* (Matthew 6:21). Your money follows your heart, and if you want to follow Jesus with all of your heart, then your money must follow Jesus.

That is financial discipleship. A financial disciple first learns to manage money and possessions God's way, applying biblical principles in every area of life – family, business, church, and social circles. Then, the financial disciple becomes an obedient teacher, committed to Jesus' command to *"Go therefore and make disciples . . . teaching them to observe all that I have commanded you"* (Matthew 28:19-20, ESV).

—

CHAPTER 1

—

What Is a Disciple?

Christians were called disciples first! This may sound a little strange as we are more used to the term "Christians" for followers of Jesus. The name "Christian" is much more popular than "disciple," but the Bible speaks much more about disciples than Christians. Most translations use the word "Christian" only three times, including, *"The disciples were called Christians first at Antioch"* (Acts 11:26).

In the first century, everyone knew what a disciple was because they were commonplace in their culture. Disciples were people who had attached themselves to a more learned, wise, or experienced person in order to learn from him. The Greek word used for disciple is *"mathetes,"* meaning, learner; the person to whom he or she was attached would be a *"didaskolos,"* meaning, teacher. The Greeks used the disciple-teacher way of educating people during the normal course of their lives, experiencing everyday happenings together. They normally lived together and shared experiences, learning from each other.

Jesus used the same method to train His disciples, who would form the nucleus of the new movement. In Greek schools of the day, the kids – disciples – did not have to sit in a classroom all day. Rather, they learned by walking around, observing and discussing with their teacher. To the Greek mind, discipleship meant following, imitating, and learning.

Mark tells us that Jesus *"appointed twelve that they might be with him and that he might send them out to preach"* (Mark 3:14). The basis of discipleship is therefore to be "with Him" in a daily relationship, to learn from Him and to be "sent out" to minister to others in the same way.

A good definition of a disciple was coined by a distant relative of mine, Stuart Briscoe. "A disciple is a person who has an ongoing, life-changing relationship with Jesus Christ and who gladly shares what he or she has learned with others."

I remember driving home from a family holiday, uncertain as to which road I should be taking. Driving out of the vacation spot, three cars were following us. Several miles later we were clearly lost and decided to drive into a parking lot to read the map and see which route we should be taking. Three cars followed us in. I asked one of the drivers if they knew the road to take.

"No," he said, "we were following you!"

I learned two lessons from this. First, if you are going to lead anyone, you need to know where you are going. Second, if you are following someone, you need to be assured that they know what they are doing!

A disciple is a learner, learning from someone with more wisdom and experience. Our ultimate teacher is, of course, Jesus Himself, but we need to attach ourselves to a disciple more advanced than we are who will help us know Jesus better. We must carefully choose who we attach ourselves to. That disciple must be following Jesus and obeying the Scriptures. Paul could say, *"Follow my example, as I follow the example of Christ"* (1 Corinthians 11:1).

A disciple is called to walk "with" Christ (evangelism), equipped to live "in" Christ (learning), sent to live "for" Christ (service), and commanded "by" Christ to minister to others (empowerment).

Some of the very last words Jesus gave His disciples after His resurrection formed a command to *"Go and make disciples . . ."* (Matthew 28:19). What they had learned from Him was to be transferred to others and reproduced.

The purpose of discipleship

Maturity in Christ is the purpose and ultimate goal of discipleship. *"He is the one we proclaim, admonishing and teaching everyone with all wisdom, so that we may present everyone fully mature in Christ"* (Colossians 1:28). The Greek word for mature is *"teleios"* meaning complete, adult, and perfect.

Developing this maturity requires a three-fold transformation. Jesus Christ performs a change that affects every area of our life. We see this transformation at three levels that are interdependent:

- Being a new person – I get a new *identity*. Christ lives in me. I live according to a new set of values: new priorities, new objectives, new hopes. I have been given a new life! *"We were therefore buried with him through baptism into death in order that, just as Christ was raised from the dead through the glory of the Father, we too may live a new life"* (Romans 6:4).

- Seeing with different eyes – I get a new *mind*. The mind of Christ molds me. He transforms our attitudes and worldview. The Holy Spirit develops in us the mind of Christ, so that we can make accurate judgments of any situation. *"The person with the Spirit makes judgments about all things, but such a person is not subject to merely human judgments, for, 'Who has known the mind of the Lord so as to instruct him?' But we have the mind of Christ"* (1 Corinthians 2:16).

- Living a new life – I get new *ethics*. The love of Christ compels me. I get not only new relationships but a new attitude toward old relationships (forgiveness, reconciliation, and peace). *"And this is his command: to believe in the name of his Son, Jesus Christ, and to love one another as he commanded us"* (1 John 3:23).

Christ develops progressively in us a new moral character that is a mirror of His own character. It is, therefore, a holistic transformation: existential, emotional, ethical, relational.

The condition of this maturity is being *"in Christ."* *"Therefore, if anyone is in Christ, he is a new creation; the old has passed away, behold, the new has come"* (2 Corinthians 5:17, RSV).

The key question is, how can this be possible? It is humanly impossible. There is a supernatural element in this life-changing experience that goes far beyond human efforts or resources. The changing power comes not only from the message of Jesus (his ideas and example) but also His power. As the blind man healed by Jesus bluntly put it, *"if this man were not from God, he could do nothing"* (John 9:33).

The main calling on our life as disciples is a continuous process of transformation into the image of Christ. Randy Alcorn stated what most people have experienced as the purpose of life. He said, "All of your life, you have been on a treasure hunt. You have been searching for a perfect person and a perfect place."

I found that perfect person, Jesus, and also the perfect place He led me to — the Kingdom of God.

A disciple follows, then leaves!

"Come, follow Me, and I will send you out to fish for people!" This invitation was given by Jesus to four men in the fishing business: Simon, Andrew, James and John. Their response? *"At once they left their nets and followed him"* (Mark 1:17-18).

They left their nets, their boats, their family, their employees, their business, and their livelihood to follow Jesus. To do this was a decision full of deep and lasting emotions. Later Simon, now Peter, exclaimed to Jesus, *"We have left everything to follow you!"*

"'Truly I tell you,' Jesus replied, 'no one who has left home or brothers or sisters or mother or father or children or fields for me and the gospel will fail to receive a hundred times as much in this present age: homes, brothers, sisters, mothers, children and fields — along with persecutions — and in the age to come eternal life" (Mark 10:28-30).

Peter's having *"left everything"* causes concern, just as it did in the story of the rich, young ruler who was called by Jesus to sell all he possessed and give it to the poor. He turned his back on Jesus and went away sad.

It may help to realize that the disciples went back to their fishing business several times during their walk with Jesus; this indicates that their family business was still intact. And Peter did not leave his wife; she later traveled with him on his mission (see 1 Corinthians 9:5).

So, what does it mean to leave everything? This means being available to leave whatever we are doing to obey Christ's call. This means cutting the umbilical cord that attaches us too strongly to our work, dreams, ambitions, and possessions. It means giving priority to Christ's commands, dropping everything to obey Him. It means placing all our money, assets, gifts, and talents into His hands – and then receiving them back to steward or manage at His direction.

I remember being at a garden party held at the beautiful home of a highly paid Italian executive. In thanking his wife for her hospitality, I remarked, "You have a wonderful home here, you must be very happy."

"Not really," she replied. "As an Italian, I really miss my family back home."

"Then why don't you go back to Italy?"

"It's not possible," she said. "We have such a high mortgage and a quite expensive lifestyle. We wouldn't be able to just pack up and leave. I'm not happy at all." Then she remarked, "It's like we are living in a golden cage."

My wife and I decided throughout our marriage to keep our living expenses as small as possible so that whenever Christ called us to do something, we would be available. I left business three times to heed His call to start a Christian movement. First, a well-paid job as a managing director of a Dutch subsidiary of an International chemical company. Then, I stopped my own business because the ministry expansion was so great. Later, in 2007, I left a highly paid job as managing director of a space services company. That would never have been possible if we had been saddled with high financial obligations. Our income took a tumble each time, but the Lord was faithful, and we have lacked nothing. I learned that God always pays for what He orders!

A disciple follows then leaves to be free to work together with Jesus in His mission.

The mission of the disciple

The practice of discipleship is to follow Jesus in His mission. He set out His mission statement in Mark 10:45, clearly declaring what he came to do. *"For even the Son of Man did not come to be served, but to serve, and to give his life as a ransom for many."*

His mission was, simply, to serve others and to set them free!

The mission of a disciple is first of all to serve. To serve means to seek the best for others and to help them achieve what is best for them. To serve is to love, and Jesus calls us *to "Love the Lord your God with all your heart and with all your soul and with all your strength and with all your mind; and, love your neighbor as yourself"* (Luke 10:27).

As disciples, we are to serve the purposes of the Lord God and obey all His commands. A natural outflowing of our service for God is to love and serve our neighbors, treating them as we would want to be treated. Service is love in action.

The second part of the mission of a disciple — following the Master — is to give your life as a ransom to set people free. Freedom has two dimensions: to be free from things that hinder us, and to be free to do what the Master wants us to do.

We can be used to set people free *from* anxiety, worries, debt, materialism, consumerism, greed, and idolatry.

Then, we can help people be free *to* know, love, and serve God and to love their neighbors. Free to be generous and content. Free to become available for the Lord's work. Free to be able to reach their life goals.

—

CHAPTER 2

—

The Cost of Discipleship

The cost of following Jesus as a disciple is not cheap. The more valuable something is, the more expensive it gets. *"Then Jesus said to his disciples, 'Whoever wants to be my disciple must deny themselves and take up their cross and follow me'"* (Matthew 16:24).

Jesus gives those wanting to be a financial disciple – learning from and following Jesus – a huge challenge. Taking up your cross daily means putting your own desires and ambitions on the altar of obedience to God. His will and plan for your life must come first, because His plan prioritizes the well-being of your soul. Anything which stands in the way of following Jesus – possessions, money, ambition, desires – must be brought to the cross and submitted. This yields an eternal reward in proportion to your obedience.

Nothing or no one is to have priority over obedience to the Master. There is no such thing as cheap discipleship. Following Jesus comes at a price. That price is the denial of self. Therefore, we need to realize the cost of following Jesus, which will inevitably lead us to a cross; the very road He took! We are challenged to hand over to the Father everything we possess so that He can use whatever we give Him for His purposes. Remember, whatever we place into His hands, He multiplies and uses for our benefit!

Jesus stated emphatically that, *"Those of you who do not give up everything you have cannot be my disciples"* (Luke 14:33).

Starting on the journey of financial discipleship means surrendering fully to the Lordship of Christ. In Luke 14, Jesus vividly describes starting with the following four steps.

1. Acknowledge that Christ IS the priority. *"If anyone comes to me and does not hate his own father and mother and wife and children and brothers and sisters, yes, and even his own life, he cannot be my disciple"* (Luke 14:26, ESV).

2. Deny yourself. *"And whoever does not carry their cross and follow me cannot be my disciple"* (Luke 14:27).

3. Count the cost. *"Suppose one of you wants to build a tower. Won't you first sit down and estimate the cost to see if you have enough money to complete it?"* (Luke 14:28).

4. Renounce all and follow Him. *"In the same way, those of you who do not give up everything you have cannot be my disciples"* (Luke 14:33).

The Lord repeatedly said, "Whoever loses their life for my sake will find it." In fact, this saying of His is found in the four Gospels more frequently than almost anything else He said. (See Matthew 10:39; 16:25; Mark 8:35; Luke 9:24; 17:33; John 12:25). Why is it repeated so often? Is it not because it sets forth one of the most fundamental principles of the Christian life, namely, that life spent for self is life lost, but life poured out for Him is life found, saved, enjoyed, and kept for eternity?

And if it can be said that the life of true discipleship is the most spiritually satisfying life in this world, it can be said with equal certainty that it will be the most rewarded in the age to come. *"For the Son of man is going to come in his Father's glory with his angels, and then he will reward each person according to what they have done"* (Matthew 16:27).

Born into a wealthy American family, William Borden attended Princeton Seminary and graduated from Yale. Despite an upper-class upbringing, his travels around the world challenged him to address the needs of the heathen world for Jesus Christ. He decided to make his choices count toward that goal.

As Borden trained for a life of service to the Kansu people of China, his heart and labor went out in very practical ways to the widows, orphans and cripples in the back streets of Chicago. A quiet yet powerful man, he diligently sought to win other young college men for Christ and His service.

His arrival in Egypt in 1913 was tragically marked by his contracting cerebral meningitis. His untimely death at the age of twenty-five was covered by nearly every newspaper in the United States as a testimony for Christ. Though a "waste" in the world's terms, both his life and his death have been a testimony and a challenge even beyond his own generation to "keep eternity's values in view."

Therefore, the truly blessed man in time and in eternity is the one who can say with William Borden, "Lord Jesus, I take my hands off, as far as my life is concerned. I put Thee on the throne in my heart. Change, cleanse, use me as Thou shalt choose."

Dallas Willard said, "The cost of non-discipleship is much higher than the cost of discipleship. Discipleship is a bargain." In other words, Jesus isn't talking about making a sacrifice simply because it's the right thing to do; he's talking about a sacrifice that actually becomes an *investment* that yields a return.

Jesus encourages us to do a cost-benefit analysis and make a wise decision. The kind of sacrifice Jesus calls us to is not something that leaves us with nothing; it's a sacrifice that becomes an investment, like planting crops that eventually yield a hundredfold return.

He's calling us to invest! He tells us to sell everything, like the merchant who found the pearl of great price and sold everything he had to "buy" the Kingdom – because it's actually worth far more than anything we currently have!

Jim Elliot, the missionary to Ecuador who lost his life at the hands of the very Indians he was serving with the gospel said, "He is no fool who gives what he cannot keep to gain what he cannot lose."

So, discipleship isn't *all* about sacrifice. Initially, it feels that way because we give up all we have to gain the Kingdom. But in the end, the life we receive is worth far more than any sacrifice we made. Going "all in" for the Kingdom of God is a fantastic deal. There is no need to diversify your portfolio. Discipleship to Jesus, in other words, is the best investment opportunity any human being ever gets.

The missionary C.T. Studd exclaimed, "If Jesus Christ be God, and He died for me, then no sacrifice I can make for him could be too great."

Could you agree with – or even sing along with – these words from the wonderful hymn by Isaac Watts, "When I Survey the Wondrous Cross"?

> Were the whole realm of nature mine
> That were an offering far too small
> Love so amazing so Divine
> Demands my soul, my life, my all!

CHAPTER 3

—

The Terms of Discipleship

Here are the terms of discipleship as laid down by the Savior of the world.

1. **A repentance and belief**

   "'The time has come,' he said. 'The kingdom of God has come near. Repent and believe the good news!'" (Mark 1:15).

   Jesus started his public ministry with a very clear call to repent – to turn from our previous ways which were diametrically opposed to the ways of the Kingdom. We need to confess our sins, accept that Jesus paid the price of this sin by His death and resurrection, and believe the great news that Jesus wants to bring to our lives. These are the terms of entry into the new Kingdom of which we become citizens.

2. **A supreme love for Jesus Christ**

   "If anyone comes to me and does not hate father and mother, wife and children, brothers and sisters – yes, even their own life – such a person cannot be my disciple" (Luke 14:26).

   This does not mean that we should have animosity or ill will in our hearts toward others, but it does mean that our love to Christ should be so great that all other loves are hatred by comparison. Actually, the most difficult clause in this passage is the expression, *"Yes, even their own life."* Self-love is one of the most stubborn hindrances to discipleship.

   Not until we are willing to lay down our very lives for Him will we be in the place where He wants us.

3. **A denial of self**

   "Whoever wants to be my disciple must deny themselves" (Matthew 16: 24).

   Denial of self is not the same as self-denial. The latter means forgoing certain foods, pleasures, or possessions. Denial of self means such complete submission to the lordship of Christ that self has no rights or authority at all. It means that "self" abdicates the throne.

It is expressed in the words of Henry Martyn, an early missionary to India and Persia. "Lord, let me have no will of my own, or consider my true happiness as depending in the smallest degree on anything that can befall me outwardly, but as consisting altogether in conformity to Thy will."

4. **A deliberate choosing of the cross**

"Then he said to them all: 'Whoever wants to be my disciple must deny themselves and take up their cross daily and follow me'" (Luke 9:23).

The cross is not some physical infirmity or mental anguish; these things are common to all men. The cross symbolises the shame, persecution, and abuse that the world heaped on the Son of God, and which the world will heap on all who choose to stand against the tide. Any believer can easily avoid the cross by being conformed to the world and its ways, but this will not allow you to follow Jesus. His path is a different one.

5. **A life spent in following Christ**

"As Jesus went on from there, he saw a man named Matthew sitting at the tax collector's booth. 'Follow me,' he told him, and Matthew got up and followed him" (Matthew 9:9).

To understand what this means, we need simply ask ourselves, what characterized the life of the Lord Jesus?

It was a life of obedience to the will of God.

It was a life lived in the power of the Holy Spirit.

It was a life of unselfish service for others.

It was a life of patience and long-suffering in the face of the gravest wrongs.

It was a life of zeal, self-control, meekness, kindness, faithfulness and devotion.

In order to be His disciples, we must walk as He walked.

6. **A fervent love for all who belong to Christ**
"By this everyone will know that you are my disciples, if you love one another" (John 13:35).

This is the love that esteems others better than oneself. It is the love that covers a multitude of sins. It is the love that suffers long and is kind. It doesn't boast and is not puffed up.

"It does not dishonor others, it is not self-seeking, it is not easily angered, it keeps no record of wrongs. Love does not delight in evil but rejoices with the truth. It always protects, always trusts, always hopes, always perseveres" (1 Corinthians 13:5-7).

Without this love, discipleship would be a cold, legalistic asceticism.

7. **An unswerving continuance in His Word**

"If you continue in my word, you are truly my disciples" (John 8: 31, RSV).

A disciple must persevere and continue on this lifetime journey. It is easy enough to start well, but the test is endurance to the end. *"No one who puts a hand to the plow and looks back is fit for the kingdom of God"* (Luke 9:62).

Obeying the Scriptures now and then will not suffice. Following Christ means constant, unquestioning obedience.

8. **A forsaking of all to follow Him**

"So likewise, whoever of you does not forsake all that he has cannot be My disciple" (Luke 14: 33, NKJV).

This is perhaps the most unpopular of all Christ's terms of discipleship. It may even prove to be the most unpopular verse in the whole Bible. Clever theologians can give you a thousand reasons why it does not mean what it says, but simple disciples drink it down eagerly, assuming that the Lord Jesus knew what He was saying. What is meant by forsaking all?

The one who forsakes all does not become lazy; he works hard to provide for current family needs. In seeking first the kingdom of God and His righteousness, he believes that he will never lack his daily necessities.

He cannot conscientiously hold on to surplus funds when souls are perishing for want of the gospel. He does not want to waste his life accumulating riches that will fall into the devil's hands when Christ returns for His saints.

He wants to obey the Lord's command not to lay up treasure on earth.

One of the lines of Frances Havergal's hymn says, "Take my silver and my gold; not a mite would I withhold." In 1878, four years after writing the hymn, Miss Havergal wrote to a friend: "The Lord has shown me another little step, and, of course, I have taken it with extreme delight. 'Take my silver and my gold' now means shipping off all my ornaments to the Church Missionary House, including a jewel cabinet that is really fit for a countess, where all will be accepted and disposed of for me . . . Nearly fifty articles are being packed up. I don't think I ever packed a box with such pleasure."

Hindrances to discipleship

William MacDonald in his book, *True Discipleship,* describes three kinds of people looking for escape routes to the extremely challenging call to discipleship.

This is illustrated in Jesus' account of three wannabe disciples who allowed other priorities to take precedence over following Christ. *"As they were walking along the road, a man said to him, 'I will follow you wherever you go.' Jesus replied, 'Foxes have dens and birds have nests, but the Son of Man has no place to lay his head.'*

"He said to another man, 'Follow me.' But he replied, 'Lord, first let me go and bury my father.' Jesus said to him, 'Let the dead bury their own dead, but you go and proclaim the kingdom of God.'

"Still another said, 'I will follow you, Lord; but first let me go back and say goodbye to my family.' Jesus replied, 'No one who puts a hand to the plow and looks back is fit for service in the kingdom of God'" (Luke 9:57-62).

We see three different individuals coming face to face with Jesus Christ and feeling an inner compulsion to follow Him. However, they permitted something else to come between their souls and complete dedication to Him.

Mr. Too Quick

The first man could be called Mr. Too Quick. He enthusiastically volunteered to follow the Lord anywhere. *"I will follow you wherever you go."* No cost would be too great. No path would be too rough.

Jesus said, *"Foxes have dens and birds have nests, but the Son of Man has no place to lay his head."* It was as though Jesus was saying, "The man claimed to be willing to follow me anywhere, but was he willing to forego the material comforts of life? Foxes have more of this world's comforts than I have. The birds have a nest they can call their own."

Was he willing to sacrifice the security and comforts of a home to follow Jesus? His love for earthly conveniences seemed to be greater than his dedication to Christ.

Mr. Too Slow

The second man could be called Mr. Too Slow.

It was not that he was completely disinterested in the Lord or refused to follow him. There was something he wanted to do first. He put his own claims above the claims of Christ.

Notice his reply, *"Lord, first let me go and bury my father."* A son should respect his parents, and if a father has died, it is certainly right to ensure a decent burial.

Apparently, he did not realize that the words "Lord . . . me first" should never be spoken after hearing a call from Jesus. If Christ is Lord, then *He* must come first. The main thrust of life must be to advance Christ's mission on earth.

It seems that the price was too great for Mr. Too Slow to pay.

If Mr. Too Quick illustrated material comforts as a hindrance to discipleship, Mr. Too Slow might refer to a job or an occupation taking precedence over the main reason for a Christian's existence. There is certainly nothing wrong in secular employment. God wants us to work in order to provide for our needs and those of the family. However, if the call comes, we must be willing to put Christ's mission first.

Mr. Too Easy

The third man could be called Mr. Too Easy. Like the first, he volunteered to follow the Lord, but like the second, he also used those forbidden words, "Lord . . . me first." He said, *"I will follow you, Lord; but first let me go back and say goodbye to my family."*

In itself, there was nothing basically wrong with his request. It is certainly not contrary to God's purposes to show a loving interest in your family. However, he allowed familial ties to supersede the place of Christ.

With penetrating insight, Jesus said, *"No one who puts a hand to the plow and looks back is fit for service in the kingdom of God."*

It was as though Jesus was saying, "I want those who follow me to be willing to renounce home ties and not be distracted by family issues; they must put me above everyone else in their lives."

Mr. Too Easy left Jesus and walked sadly down the road. His overconfident aspirations to be a disciple had dashed themselves to pieces on the rocks of congenial family bonds.

We see here three primary hindrances to true discipleship.

Mr. Too Quick – the love of earthly comforts
Mr. Too Slow – the precedence of a job or occupation
Mr. Too Easy – the priority of family ties

Throughout my life, I have met these three people several times! The young couple who placed home comforts above Christ's call. The young business guy, a high-potential leader, who considered his career to be a higher calling than "the upward call" of Jesus. The businessman who could not leave his place in the family business even though it was almost killing him spiritually and relationally.

We should not become discouraged in our disciple-making. Our task is to make the claims of Christ known and clear. It is sad that many people, on whom we have pinned our hopes, should decide that the cost is too great.

The Lord Jesus still calls, as He has ever called, for men and women to follow Him heroically and sacrificially.

PART 1: DISCIPLESHIP

—

CHAPTER 4

—

Disciples Are Stewards

"Each of you should use whatever gift you have received to serve others, as faithful stewards of God's grace in its various forms" (1 Peter 4:10).

In modern church life, the term "stewardship" has become largely associated with giving money, but not so in the Bible. Everything we have – not only money, but also life, time, talents, and especially the great gift of God's grace in all of its fullness – has been committed to us in trust from God, to be used for Him. We are His stewards, and the Bible's use of the word means a trusted servant to whom his master has committed the management of his household, his business affairs, and even the education of his children. Everything was "delegated" into the steward's care by his master.

"This, then, is how you ought to regard us: as servants of Christ and as those entrusted with the mysteries God has revealed" (I Corinthians 4:1).

A minister of Christ is to be a steward entrusted with what Paul calls *"the mysteries God has revealed"*: secret and hidden wisdom of God, valuable truths found nowhere but in the revelation of the Word of God. Financial disciples, as stewards, are responsible to dispense these remarkable truths about life to the people they serve so that their lives and behavior are changed. These mysteries, when understood, are the basis upon which all of God's purposes in our life are worked out.

Five mysteries

What are these mysteries, or secrets? Here are my top five:

1. The mystery of the Kingdom of God

> *"The secret of the kingdom of God has been given to you. But to those on the outside everything is said in parables"* (Mark 4:11).

This involves understanding God at work in history, how he is working through the events of our day and days past, and how he uses events that fill our media to carry out his purposes. This mystery explains our ability to influence the kingdoms of this world with the Kingdom of God, bringing light to a dark world.

2. The mystery of iniquity or unrighteousness

"For the mystery of lawlessness is already at work" (2 Thessalonians 2:7, ESV).

We desperately need to understand why we are never able to make any progress when it comes to solving human dilemmas — why every generation without exception repeats the struggles, problems, and difficulties of the previous generation — why no lessons are learned from the crises we endure.

For financial disciples, money is described as "worldly wealth" in Luke 16:11. In Greek this is *"mammonas tes adikias."* Literally translated, this means "mammon of iniquity," which describes the power behind money that moves us to make wrong choices, serving money instead of serving God. A financial disciple has to understand the power behind money and use it to promote God's Kingdom over the desires of the flesh.

3. The mystery of godliness

"Beyond all question, the mystery from which true godliness springs is great" (1 Timothy 3:16).

This is the remarkable secret that God has provided by which a Christian is enabled to live righteously in the pressures of this world with all of its illusion, temptations, and danger — not running away from it but refusing to conform to it and doing so in a loving, gracious way. It is the secret of an imparted life: *"Christ in you, the hope of glory"* (Colossians 1:27). Christ in you, available to you — His life, His wisdom, His strength, His power to act — enabling you to do what you do not think you can do. That is the mystery of holiness, the most life-transforming doctrine that has ever been set before man, radical in its effect.

4. The mystery of the church

"This mystery is that the Gentiles are fellow heirs, members of the same body, and partakers of the promise in Christ Jesus through the gospel" (Ephesians 3:6, ESV).

The Church – that strange new society that God is building – is a demonstration to a watching world of a totally different lifestyle. It is to repel the impact of the world upon it, being instead an impact upon the world around it. The foundation for entrance into the church is faith in Jesus' work on the cross.

5. The mystery of the gospel

"Pray also for me, that words may be given to me in opening my mouth boldly to proclaim the mystery of the gospel, for which I am an ambassador in chains, that I may declare it boldly, as I ought to speak" (Ephesians 6:19-20, ESV).

We are to be a channel through which the gospel flows. Stewardship is based on the gospel. It is the process of integrating the gospel into every area of life. In a day when the world seems to have lost hope, the gospel is still "good news."

In lives desperately seeking understanding and hope, the gospel still brings a new reality. Where sin binds human hearts and lives, the gospel still has the power to shatter the chains that bind them. And we are stewards of this good news.

Stewardship

This can be explained as the three legs of a stool. Each leg must be stable and equal if the stool is to stand.

The first leg of the stool is God's ownership of everything. He is creator and sustainer of the whole universe and has never relinquished His ownership. *"Every animal in the forest belongs to me, and so do the cattle on a thousand hills. I know all the birds in the mountains, and every wild creature is in my care. If I were hungry, I wouldn't tell you, because I own the world and everything in it"* (Psalm 50:10-12, CEV).

The second leg is that God has redeemed us. Having bought us for a great price, we and everything in our possession or under our control belong to Him. *"You are not your own; you were bought at a price. Therefore, honor God with your bodies"* (1 Corinthians 6:19b-20). We do not own anything, but that's good news, because if we don't own anything, we can't lose anything!

The third leg of the stool is God's invitation to become managers of His property and all the resources He gives us. *"You made them rulers over the works of your hands; you put everything under their feet"* (Psalm 8:6). What a wonderful privilege, and what an awesome responsibility!

One Sunday, an older gentleman had finished the Compass course "Navigating Your Finances – God's Way." He thanked the leader of his group and said to him, "The one thing in this entire study that has had the single greatest impact on me was the idea that God owns everything, including me." He went on to say, "I have been in the church all my life, but somehow never realized this. I thought I'm the one going to work; I'm the one making the money. It's mine to do with whatever I want. But when I realized God owns me and everything I have, it changed everything in my life!"

"Now I realize that under God's ownership every spending decision becomes a spiritual decision. I no longer ask, 'Lord, what do You want me to do with my money?' I ask a different question, 'Lord, what do You want me to do with Your money?'"

As a steward, your life and possessions are no longer about *you*. Everything is about fulfilling God's purposes with the resources He gives you to utilize.

There is a lot written and taught about the stewardship of resources, money, and possessions, and we will certainly touch on these in this book. However, the need of the hour is to steward relationships the way Jesus did — advancing the gospel through making disciples.

PART 1: DISCIPLESHIP

—

CHAPTER 5

—

Disciples Make Disciples

Following Christ means to make other disciples, just like He did. His words echo throughout the ages, *"Go therefore and make disciples . . ."* The highest priority isn't having daily devotions, learning how to manage money, or doing business God's way; it's to *make disciples*.

The reality is that we have always been involved in disciple-making: it just hasn't always been disciple-making for Jesus. You *are* a disciple; you are following someone. The question is, who is following you? You *have* disciples, people watching you daily. How are you influencing the people watching you? Every one of us follows someone, and every one of us carries significant influence over someone else. Disciple-making begins at home with our spouse and our children, at work with our colleagues, and at play with our friends.

In my last job as the CEO of a space services business, we employed about 85 high-tech professionals. I considered each one of them a "pre-disciple," because I wanted them to learn from me what Jesus would do. As the CEO, I knew I was working in a kind of glass house. Everyone in our business was looking at me — how I work, how I deal with people, conflicts, and challenges. A guiding biblical principle was, *"Let your light shine before others, that they may see your good deeds and glorify your Father in heaven"* (Matthew 5:16). My prayer was that when people watch me working, they may be pointed to Christ.

The New Zealander Paul Gilbert wrote this rhyme.

> You are writing a Gospel
> A chapter each day
> By deeds that you do
> By words that you say.
> Men read what you write
> Whether faithless or true
> Say, what is the Gospel
> According to you?

We have been called to follow Jesus, so we want to help others follow Him. We are not asking disciples to follow us. Even Paul didn't want

Christians to follow him but rather to follow his example as stated in 1 Corinthians 11:1. *"Follow my example, as I follow the example of Christ."* We don't want to be leaders with many followers; we want to be servants who help many follow Christ. We disciple others because we want something *for* them, not because we something *from* them.

It all started by Jesus calling twelve men to follow Him. His concern was not programs to reach the multitudes but men whom the multitudes would follow. These twelve and those they would teach were to be His method of winning the world to His Father. Jesus started to gather these men before He preached in public.

The initial objective of Jesus' plan was to enlist men who could bear witness to His life and carry on His work after He returned to the Father.

It is interesting to observe that Jesus' disciple-making had little or no immediate effect upon the religious life of His day, but that did not matter so much. These few early converts were destined to become the leaders of His Church that would take the gospel to the entire world. The significance of their lives would be felt throughout eternity.

What is more revealing about these men is that they do not impress us at first as being key men. For the most part they were common working men. None occupied prominent places in society. They were impulsive, temperamental, easily offended, and had all the religious prejudices of their society. One might have wondered how Jesus could ever use these guys. This was certainly not the kind of group you would expect to win the world for Christ! Yet, Jesus saw in these simple men the potential of leadership for the Kingdom.

They were *"unlearned and ignorant"* according to the world's standard (Acts 4:13, KJV). Though often mistaken in their judgment and slow to comprehend spiritual things, they were honest men, willing to confess their need . . . and they were teachable!

Perhaps most significant about them was their sincere desire for God and the realities of His way of life. They were fed up with the hypocrisy of the ruling aristocracy. Some of them had already joined the revival movement of John the Baptist (John 1:35). These men were looking for someone to lead them in the way of salvation. Jesus can use anyone who wants to be used.

The wisdom of His method was the fundamental principle of concentrating on those He intended to use. One cannot transform the world without transforming individuals. Individuals cannot be changed except as they are molded in the hands of the Master.

Jesus deliberately portioned His time to those He wanted to train, demonstrating a fundamental principle of making disciples: the more concentrated the size of the group being taught, the greater the opportunity for effective instruction. He ministered to the crowds but taught the few. Jesus was not trying to impress the crowds but to usher in a kingdom. Since this meant He needed people who could lead multitudes, he devoted himself primarily to a few so that the masses could at last be saved.

Having called His men, Jesus made a practice of being with them. The essence of His training program? He just let His disciples follow Him. That's all! Jesus' way was incredibly simple. No formal school, no seminaries, no outlined course to study, none of the highly organized procedures considered so necessary today.

Amazingly, all Jesus did to teach these men was to draw them close to Himself. Jesus was His own school; He was the curriculum.

The basic principle of making disciples is *"that they might be with him"* (Mark 3:14). There is simply no substitute for doing life together with people. The friend/mentor/counselor should stay with the new believer as much as possible, studying the Bible and praying with them, answering questions, clarifying the truth, and seeking together to help others.

The only way to effectively train such leaders is to give them a leader to follow.

When discussing Jesus' choice of twelve men as His disciples, we should also realize that many women followed and learned from Him. "*Soon afterward he went on through cities and villages, proclaiming and bringing the good news of the kingdom of God. And the twelve were with him, and also some women who had been healed of evil spirits and infirmities: Mary, called Magdalene, from whom seven demons had gone out, and Joanna, the wife of Chuza, Herod's household manager, and Susanna, and many others, who provided for them out of their means*" (Luke 8:1-3, ESV). These women also supported Jesus' ministry financially. That's what disciples do.

I have been privileged to know three godly women who were disciple-makers and who influenced my life greatly. Corrie ten Boom was imprisoned by the Nazis in a concentration camp and is well known for forgiving her brutal camp guard, whom she met again after the war ended. Her life was dedicated to bringing people to Jesus, and she left an everlasting inheritance. She said, "You can never learn that Christ is all you need, until Christ is all you have."

Gien Karssen is less well known, but she stood tall at the very beginning of the ministry of The Navigators in The Netherlands. She discipled many women and influenced great numbers of men in their walk with Christ. Her life was characterized by three things found in her writings: "a great love for God, a deep respect for His Word, and a passion to share my life with others."

Last but not least is my wife, Didie, who has been discipling me for about 50 years. I am a slow learner!

Jesus' way – four environments

Jesus was, of course, the perfect discipler. He had perfect love, perfect purpose, and a perfect method to train His people. If we follow His method, we can be assured of God's blessing in our disciple-making.

Jesus' method occurs in four different environments: the large group, the small group, the inner circle, and time alone with God. These four environments are just as crucial for disciple-makers today.

I want to unpack these four environments by describing five principles I learned from Kent Humphreys, then president of the Fellowship of Companies for Christ, of which my business was a member. He modeled these principles as he discipled businesspeople. I followed Kent because he followed Jesus.

1. Jesus told everyone to respond to the Good News.

Whenever Jesus came into a community, He told everyone the good news. That is why people immediately surrounded Him. We as the church today are doing a good job of sharing the good news of Jesus Christ through evangelism, church services, videos, newspapers, radio, television, internet, magazines, tracts, and so forth. Jesus told everyone. *"Go into all the world and preach the gospel to all creation"* (Mark 16:15). This is the largest group of all.

2. Jesus taught many to understand God's principles.

Jesus had other large groups – congregations listening to His teaching. He taught not only in the synagogues but also on the hillsides with more than five thousand people in a single setting. He said that He was teaching for the purpose of understanding. Teaching provides an atmosphere that stimulates thinking. It answers the questions of *who* is to do the ministry and *what* they are to do. It is a mental exercise that can result in personal change; when less effective it results in just more knowledge. But it is always the starting point for change. *"Again Jesus called the crowd to him and said, 'Listen to me, everyone, and understand this'"* (Mark 7:14).

We have no lack of good teaching in our churches, conferences, online outlets, books, videos, etc. The church today is not only telling everyone the good news, we are probably doing a better job of teaching than we have ever done.

3. Jesus trained some to do the work.

Jesus trained at least seventy people to go out and actually do the work. *"The Lord now chose seventy-two other disciples and sent them ahead in pairs to all the towns and places he planned to visit"* (Luke 10:1, NLT). He told them, *"The harvest is plentiful, but the workers are few. Ask the Lord of the harvest, therefore, to send out workers into his harvest field."* (Luke 10:2).

The process He employed went like this: He told a truth so they could hear it, He taught them something so they could understand it, and He trained them so they could do it. An old truth says, "Telling is not teaching. Listening is not learning. You learn to do by doing." In other words, just telling someone something doesn't mean we are teaching him. Just because he is listening doesn't mean he is learning. People learn to do by doing. Training has to do with doing.

Training provides an atmosphere in which individual change happens in a small group setting. Those involved are emotionally engaged in relationships with others in the training process. To many of you, training means a weekend seminar where you go for a day, or maybe a training seminar during the week. There may be some teaching at these events, but training involves learning how and when to do the things you have been taught. It involves actually going and doing.

If a pastor is a teaching pastor but is not enabling people to be trained by either him or someone else in his church, he is only accomplishing one aspect of what Jesus did. If a pastor is an evangelist and is on the radio and on television and is passing out tracts and telling many people the good news but is not taking the people to the next step of teaching or the further step of training, then he is not completing what Jesus asked him to do. So, who are you training in your church? Jesus told everyone, he taught many, he trained some.

Notice that as the size of the group decreases, there is less organization and more opportunity for relationship. When you are telling everyone in a large group context, there is no opportunity for personal relationship.

If you are teaching many, you can teach principles, but you cannot have a personal relationship with each individual. When you start training, you have less organization and deeper relationship. Finally, when you go to one-on-one equipping, you have very high relationship and extremely little organization.

We have a problem in our church's model today because we haven't followed the model of Jesus. We are heavy on organization and large-group structures, but we are not heavy on relationship that develops through small-group training.

A friend of mine told me just today that he was in a church situation where the elders met regularly but had no strong relationship with each other. When a crisis came, they were organizational, but they were not relational. Most problems in your church have little to do with the organization or structure; problems are generally about relationships. The reason we have relationship problems in our churches is because we are telling everyone, we are teaching many, we are training some, but we are not doing a good job of equipping or of modeling a personal relationship with God.

4. Jesus equipped a few to reproduce.

The fourth thing Jesus did was to equip a few to reproduce.

Jesus set the pattern of equipping a very small group of twelve and spending additional time and effort with only three. Equipping happens, I believe, within a group of one to twelve. Jesus gave us the model of the twelve because you cannot equip a leader in a large group setting. The Greek word for equipping is first seen in Mark chapter one and is translated "mending the nets." It means to take something that is not functioning and make it useable. That is what we are trying to do. When we equip people, we are taking poorly functioning people from the pews and helping them function correctly to be used by God. They are motivated as they learn to make spiritual choices and as their questions of the where and why of the spiritual walk are answered.

In Mark 14:33, Jesus demonstrated yet another style: He took three of the disciples — Peter, James, and John — and shared privately with them. This was His inner circle in whom He invested more time than He did with the other nine disciples. Many of His most trying moments were with these men. In fact, Peter would deny Him three times. Jesus obviously believed that this intimate method of influence was worth the time, and even Peter proved this to be true when he became the vibrant leader of the first-century church.

As Jesus equipped Peter, James, and John, they became His most intimate friends. They are the men He wanted close when His life took its hardest turn, the Garden of Gethsemane.

Who are you giving your life to? Who are the people in your inner circle? When you approach the storms of life, who will you turn to? Are there three people you would immediately call if you had a crisis in your life? Are there three people who care for your soul and who would minister to you? It may take you several years of relationships to find the people who will be in an inner circle, but every one of us needs to have a Peter, James, and John in our life. Pray for such people and seek them out. They may be people other than those you are equipping; they may not even live in your city. But find these folks and nurture these relationships.

5.   Jesus modeled a relationship with the Father.

The goal of all spiritual teaching and training and equipping is to enable men and women to walk with Jesus Christ. The focus is not on your mind, not on your emotion or even your will; it is on your heart motives. When others watch your life, what do they see? Do you let them get close enough to see you as you really are? Jesus allowed the disciples to be close enough to see Him in His moment of crisis so that they could see His relationship with the Father.

If you are a leader in the body of Christ, people are watching your life. They want to see how you react when things go well and how you handle life when you go through a crisis.

They watched what Jesus did in the crisis. They watched the relationship between the Father and the Son. Four times in John 17, Jesus' last prayer on behalf of His precious disciples, He prayed *"that they may be one."* He desired unity for them, and He allowed them to get close enough to Him that they learned by His model. Do you want unity in your church, business, government, family, and community? Be a model of a person whose heart is wholly God's, and He will create unity.

It is easy to say that Jesus was perfect, so of course He wouldn't mind the disciples getting close. But who among us wants people close enough to see that we are not perfect? God hasn't asked perfection of us. He has only asked for a seeking heart, one that fears the Lord. That heart He will honor, and that heart in a person will bring others closer to God.

Finally, notice that in Mark 14:35, Jesus left the three and fell on His face before His Father. The Gospel accounts frequently record Jesus leaving the disciples to spend time with His Father in prayer.

"Where is the man who fears the Lord? God will teach him how to choose the best. He shall live within God's circle of blessing, and his children shall inherit the earth. Friendship with God is reserved for those who reverence him. With them alone he shares the secrets of his promises" (Psalm 25:12-14, TLB).

Where is the man or woman who fears the Lord? God will teach him or her how to choose the best. Are you allowing people to see you choose the best? Are you allowing them to see the heart motives in your life? When others watch your life, what do they see? Do you let them get close enough to see you as you really are?

The disciples must have felt as though they were floundering when Jesus ascended to heaven. Now that He was no longer with them in the flesh every day, it was probably a nervous and maybe even fearful time. Jesus knew they were ready, but experience had not yet proved it to them. Still, they knew they could depend on what they had seen Him do, the things He had taught them, and the guidance of the Spirit that He had recently sent. His model was their greatest comfort.

Your disciples, too, will experience much the same as you release them to duplicate this process in their own relationships. You have been with them regularly for a long time. Now you will begin a new group, and they will reproduce what you have taught them. They are now the mentors, the teachers. Jesus' model will again provide comfort. Help them to understand it before you release them.

—

CHAPTER 6

—

Characteristics of a Disciple

"Ooh, cotton candy!" I was at the funfair with my small daughter as she looked longingly at that big, pink, fluffy spinning mass of sugar. The seller held out a stick of cotton candy that was bigger than my daughter's head.

"How can such a little girl like you eat such a big cotton candy?" he asked.

"Well, that's easy," said my little girl. "I am much bigger inside than outside!"

When managing our money, we are always tightly focused on externals: our job, bills to be paid, desires to be met, investments to follow, an uncertain future to deal with. But it is much more important to focus first on internals, because they will determine how well we deal with the externals. Consider an iceberg: we are naturally interested in what we see – what's above the surface. We focus on tools and techniques to improve our financial state, income, expenses, etc. And that's good, of course, but it's only the tip of the iceberg. Under the water lies a much larger mass we don't see. The area under water of our financial life is our character, our motivations, our values, and our dreams.

While we naturally focus on "out-stances" (outward circumstances), we need to focus on "in-stances," (how we are within). What is within comes out! Our internal bookkeeping will determine our outward activity.

"And now, dear brothers and sisters, one final thing. Fix your thoughts on what is true, and honorable, and right, and pure, and lovely, and admirable. Think about things that are excellent and worthy of praise. ⁹ Keep putting into practice all you learned and received from me—everything you heard from me and saw me doing. Then the God of peace will be with you" (Philippians 4:8-9, NLT).

Being is more important than doing. First of all, I need to organize my life; only when that is done do I move on to determine how much money I need to finance it. I need to learn who I am, what motivates me, and what I really want from life.

This is where being a follower of Jesus gives us great advantages. A Christian is not better than anyone else, but a Christian is much better off! We have the Holy Spirit dwelling in us, bringing all the resources of God Himself into our lives. *"For God gave us a spirit not of fear but of power and love and self-control"* (2 Timothy 1:7, ESV).

We receive power to overcome temptations, to work effectively, to build up our resources, to defeat the power of money. We receive love to serve God and our neighbor, to use our money for good, and to share freely. We receive self-control to be disciplined with our spending and saving, to think in the right way from a sound mind about our financial dealings, and to live moderately, enjoying God's provision.

Here are some important life characteristics of a faithful and reliable disciple that can help us evaluate whether our lives correspond to what the Lord is expecting from us.

1. A faithful and reliable disciple spends time in God's Word.

Last week I was doing what most men don't do – looking at an instruction manual! I had a small problem with my car and went to the garage for maintenance. It turned out that something in the engine needed replacing.

"Have you been checking your oil level regularly?" the mechanic asked. I hadn't, and it cost me more than I had anticipated.

When you buy a new car, television, or phone, an instruction manual comes with it. For example, the instruction manual for many cars says, "Change the oil every 3,000 miles." I can say, "Who is Ford or Toyota to tell me that I have to change the oil every 3,000 miles? I'm a free man, I can do what I want. This is my car, so I'm going to change the oil every 9,000 miles." Can you imagine what will happen to me? I won't have a car for long.

The instruction manual is for your benefit, not to give you headaches. It's for things to work well in your life. If you follow the instructions in the manual, you will be a happy man with a car for many years to come. If you don't follow them, you will suffer the consequences.

In the same way, God gave you an instruction manual when He built you. If you obey it, things will go well for you. It's not that God wants to make you suffer or make life impossible for you; rather, He wants you to benefit from obeying His Holy Word.

It is important to understand how God works. Proverbs 3:5-6 says, *"Trust in the Lord with all your heart and lean not on your own understanding; in all your ways submit to him, and he will make your paths straight."*

So, how does God work? When you abide by the principles He has for the functioning of your finances, things will go well for you – not by magic, but by observing the principles from the Bible that God has for your life. If you obey them, things will be much better for you than if you disobey them. If you change the oil in your car every 3,000 miles, it will perform better for you because that is a proper principle for taking care of your car.

The problem with many of us is that changing the oil in our car every 3,000 miles may not seem to make much sense when the oil still looks good or we don't have money to make the change. We have to put our priorities in order, saying yes to the right things and no to other things, because cheap can turn out to be expensive.

We must study the Bible, read financial books, and learn what God's recommendations are. He wants us to have a plan to control our spending, to live a life without debt, to be honest and upright, to control our standard of living, to be generous, to plan for later age, and to know how to transfer an inheritance to the next generation.

2. A faithful and reliable disciple lives an examined life.

This practice of testing your life is described in 2 Corinthians 13:5, *"Examine yourselves to see whether you are in the faith; test yourselves . . ."* Referring to the Lord's supper, Paul said, *"Everyone ought to examine themselves before they eat of the bread and drink from the cup"* (1 Corinthians 11:28).

Jeremiah admonished his people with the words, *"Let us examine our ways and test them, and let us return to the Lord"* (Lamentations 3:40).

Financial disciples should regularly test their motives, thoughts, and attitudes to check how effectively they are carrying out their responsibilities. Unfortunately, we tend to examine our lives only when things go wrong or when we are faced with a crisis. Crisis investigation is better than no investigation, but a faithful and reliable disciple makes a habit of regularly evaluating himself as part of his daily life.

The faithful and reliable disciple is like a pilot who regularly checks his flight path, making constant small corrections to stay on course. We must constantly evaluate our ways so we can correct them in alignment with the Lord's will for our lives.

Socrates concluded, "An unexamined life is not worth living."

Is your life an examined life?

3. A faithful and reliable disciple leads a controlled life.

Self-control is the last of the fruits of the Spirit (Galatians 5:23). In his letter to Titus, Paul repeats several times that believers must lead a controlled life. For example, Paul asked Titus to teach that elders must keep their lives under control (Titus 2:2), and that young women should also control their lives (Titus 2:1-6).

Paul used the discipline and self-control of an athlete to illustrate the controlled life of a disciple: *"I discipline my body like an athlete, training it to do what it should"* (1 Corinthians 9:24-27, NLT).

Solomon gives an illustrative principle when he says, *"A person without self-control is like a city with broken-down walls"* (Proverbs 25:28, NLT). Protection is gone and the city is open to all kinds of attack. Temptations work on our inability to control our desires, our tongues, and our expenses.

The faithful and reliable disciple is constantly focused on controlling his or her natural impulses – to control all desires, good or bad. He is learning not to live for the world's enticements. *"Do not love the world or anything in the world. If anyone loves the world, love for the Father is not in them. For everything in the world – the lust of the flesh, the lust of the eyes, and the pride of life – comes not from the Father but from the world. The world and its desires pass away, but whoever does the will of God lives forever"* (1 John 2:15-17).

John Milton said, "He who rules his passions, desires and fears is more than a king!"

Is your life a controlled life?

4. A faithful and reliable disciple lives a sacrificial life.

We simply cannot be reliable and faithful disciples if we do not sacrifice our lives. At the beginning of Romans 12, Paul challenges us not to conform to the ways of the world but to offer ourselves as a living sacrifice.

Jesus challenges every disciple in Luke 9:23, *"If anyone would come after me, let him deny himself and take up his cross daily and follow me"* (ESV).

In Jesus' day, the cross was used for only one purpose – to kill someone. The image he gives us of taking up our cross is rather dramatic, but it is not about a one-time sacrificial death for a good cause; the sacrifice he's talking about is a daily sacrifice! Every day we have to give up our wishes, our desires, our plans, our comfort, our hopes, and our leisure time for the cause of the Kingdom and the world we wish to serve.

John gives us in 1 John 3:16 an indication of how far we should go in sacrifice. He states, *"This is how we know what love is: Jesus Christ laid down his life for us. And we ought to lay down our lives for our brothers and sisters."* If our life is the ultimate sacrifice that may one day be asked of us, then this puts into a different context the modest sacrifice of giving our money and our time – which we manage but do not own – for the benefit of others.

If we want to be faithful and reliable disciples and hear from Jesus the words, *"Well done, good and faithful servant,"* we must first test ourselves regularly to make sure we are on the right course, the one determined by the Master. Then, we need to control our desires and impulses to make sure they don't control us. Finally, we generously and regularly give what we have under our control in the hope that we will bring a little bit of heaven to those who are here on earth.

Are you living a self-sacrificing life?

5. A faithful and reliable disciple lives a fruitful life.

The model for fruitfulness is God. After creating the universe in a magnificent display of His extravagance, **He turned to His living creatures and said,** *"Be fruitful and multiply"* (Genesis 1:28, NLT).

Reading this, we first think of generational fruitfulness – reproduction of our kind, both biological and spiritual. Some are not able to reproduce biologically, but all are challenged to reproduce spiritually. We see this kind of spiritual reproduction in Paul's example with Timothy and the next generations. *"And the things you have heard me say in the presence of many witnesses entrust to reliable people who will also be qualified to teach others"* (2 Timothy 2:2).

Priscilla and Aquila first met Paul in Corinth, where they became good friends with him and shared in his work. When Paul left, the couple stayed in Ephesus and established a church in their home (1 Corinthians 16:19). Then an eloquent preacher named Apollos came through Ephesus. Apollos knew the Scriptures, but he didn't know the significance of Christ's death and resurrection, the ministry of the indwelling Holy Spirit, or the mystery of the church. Priscilla and her husband took Apollos aside and explained these things to him (Acts 18:24-26). Both Aquila and Priscilla possessed an in-depth understanding of doctrine learned from Paul, and this husband and wife team was able to pass it on to another Christian and build him up in the faith.

There is also a fruitfulness through the traits of Christian character as produced by the Holy Spirit in our lives. *"But the fruit of the Spirit is love, joy, peace, forbearance, kindness, goodness, faithfulness, gentleness and self-control"* (Galatians 5:22-23).

Finally, there is a productive fruitfulness, using our gifts and talents together with the resources God has provided for us. This, too, is an expression of the work of the Holy Spirit through us. *"See, I have chosen Bezalel son of Uri, the son of Hur, of the tribe of Judah, and I have filled him with the Spirit of God, with wisdom, with understanding, with knowledge and with all kinds of skills – to make artistic designs for work in gold, silver and bronze, to cut and set stones, to work in wood, and to engage in all kinds of crafts"* (Exodus 31:2-5).

Jesus Christ said, *"Seek first his kingdom and his righteousness, and all these things will be given to you as well"* (Matthew 6:33). Once we learn what God's principles are for our finances, then we must be committed to obeying them; He will take care of the rest. Learning how God works and obeying Him is very important in the process of financial healing, both in personal and family life.

—

CHAPTER 7

—

Why Financial Discipleship?

Money is, of course, the language of the world. I believe God's Word is the translation of that language that leads to true financial freedom. Jesus himself explained what the source of true freedom is. He said, *". . . If you hold to my teaching, you are really my disciples. Then you will know the truth, and the truth will set you free"* (John 8:31-32). A financial disciple applies what the Bible has to say about handling money and possessions. The disciple will follow Jesus' teachings and His example and be set free to experience the adventure of financial discipleship.

A financial disciple looks for three outcomes. First, to know Christ more intimately. This means experientially — not just knowing the Bible in our head — but experiencing the living power of Jesus Himself as He lives in us and through us. The second outcome is being free to serve Him: free from debt, free from worries, and free from anxiety so that we can be free to serve wherever He would call us. The third outcome is to help fund the great commission: helping people grow in generosity so that they can finance the work of the church in fulfilling its mission.

The Lord's commission to us is to *"Go and make disciples . . . teaching them to obey everything I have commanded you"* (Matthew 28:19-20). If we are not teaching people how to handle their finances God's way, then we are omitting a large part of His teaching. Our commission is to make disciples. Managing money affects almost every area of our lives — areas in which we need to excel as disciples. It affects what we eat, how we dress, our recreation, and relationships. Money spent in one area affects what we can spend in another. There are significant psychological consequences, such as stress and anxiety, associated with money. It affects our well-being and our ability to contribute to the well-being of others. Money touches all aspects of how we live, how we think, how we feel, and what we dream. It can also cause relationship breakdowns and lead to lying and stealing.

Many of us grow up learning that money is one of a few topics — like politics, sex, and religion — that you should avoid at all costs in polite conversation. Although we're discouraged from talking about money at every turn, talking about it is necessary if we want to fix our financial situation.

Forces like social taboos, the intimidation factor, and embarrassment conspire to keep us from talking about money and improving our circumstances. "There are few things that can cause joy, shame, contentment, anxiety, and stress the way money does," said Korrena Bailie, a financial journalist. "If your finances cause you stress and anxiety, it's natural to want to keep this to yourself because you might feel embarrassed or ashamed about the decisions you made," she said. "When you ignore your financial situation, minor problems happening on a regular basis build up to very substantial challenges."

Failing to integrate biblical teaching into our financial life leads to a crucial part of our life not being influenced by the Spirit of God.

Therefore, we need to preach, teach, and model financial discipleship. Financial discipleship means:

- honoring God as the owner of everything (Lordship)
  being good stewards of His resources (Stewardship)

- sharing what we are entrusted with for His purposes (Generosity)

- passing on what we have learned to others (Discipleship)

It is a calling for believers to use God-given resources (time, money, talents, possessions, etc.) for His purposes, in His way, and for His glory. A lack of understanding about biblical stewardship is hurting Christians and churches in multiple ways. Money management is not merely a technical exercise: it is a spiritual discipline. Following Jesus in our financial life should be a major topic of learning for all believers. A healthy and bible-based financial teaching program has a huge impact on spiritual growth: it is an essential, if not critical, path of discipleship.

Man's economy is all too ready to impose its practices of debt, materialism, and the culture of "want it now" on us all. As a consequence, ministry and service suffer, leading to a loss of spiritual vitality as people struggle financially.

The term financial discipleship refers to the impact money can have on our discipleship journey. Your relationship to money will always impact your relationship with God.

Let's look at eight strong reasons why disciples need to get a biblical perspective on their relationship to money and possessions.

1. Money is a very important topic in the Bible, and God gives us a clear perspective on how to manage our finances. In fact, God talks about money nearly 2,400 times in the Bible, which is more than double the amount of times He talks about faith and love combined. So, it is extremely important in God's eyes.

2. In addition to money being an important topic to God, Jesus talked a lot about money while on earth. Fifteen percent of everything He said, including over forty percent of His parables, mentioned money and possessions. Other than the mentions of His Father and the Kingdom, Jesus is recorded in the Gospels as talking more about money than any other topic.

3. Money is a major competitor for our devotion, seeking to divert us away from God. *"No one can serve two masters. Either you will hate the one and love the other, or you will be devoted to the one and despise the other. You cannot serve both God and money"* (Matthew 6:24).

4. Money problems choke the Word and make it unfruitful as evidenced in the parable of the sower. *"Still others, like seed sown among thorns, hear the word; but the worries of this life, the deceitfulness of wealth and the desires for other things come in and choke the word, making it unfruitful"* (Mark 4:18-19). If we are not following Jesus with our finances, the Bible can become ineffective in our lives.

5. The way we use our money is an outside indicator of an inside spiritual state. *"For where your treasure is, there your heart will be also"* (Matthew 6:21). Talking about money in church is a taboo in most nations around the world. Our financial affairs are very private. However, the way we manage our money is a clear indication of our heart's devotion. If we do not teach biblical finances, then we are not touching the priorities of people's hearts!

6. The love of money lies at the root of all kinds of evil. *"For the love of money is a root of all kinds of evil. Some people, eager for money, have wandered from the faith and pierced themselves with many griefs"* (1 Timothy 6:10). Love of money leads to all kinds of wrong choices that can lead us into evil. Obvious examples include gambling, cheating, stealing, lying, manipulating.

7. Inability to pay back debt robs you of your freedom. *"The rich rule over the poor, and the borrower is slave to the lender"* (Proverbs 22:7). Just miss a payment, and the creditor will tell you who has first call on your money. You will experience the power wielded by creditors. God deserves first call on the money under our management.

8. Not knowing God's ways of handling money can harm our walk with Jesus. *"My people are destroyed from lack of knowledge . . ."* (Hosea 4:6). There is very little teaching on money and possessions in our churches. As a result, people suffer from lack of knowledge and miss God's best for their lives.

—

CHAPTER 8

—

Financial Freedom

The goal of financial discipleship is to learn, apply, and teach what the Bible has to say about handling money and possessions. Through this we experience people being set free by a deeper understanding of how God's economy operates. A guideline for me throughout my journey in financial discipleship and making disciples has been the example of Ezra. Upon arriving back in Jerusalem after exile to Babylon, Ezra reveals his priorities, *"For Ezra had set his heart to study the Law of the Lord, and to do it and to teach his statutes and rules in Israel* (Ezra 7:10, ESV). We cannot teach what we have not applied, and we cannot apply what we have not learned. We can only take people as far as we have gone. A friend of mine stated clearly, "If it doesn't work at home, don't export it!"

We want to help people become free from the power of money. Jesus stated very clearly, *"No one can serve two masters, for either he will hate the one and love the other, or he will be devoted to the one and despise the other. You cannot serve God and money"* (Matthew 6:24, ESV). Financial freedom has two dimensions: free *from* and free *to*. We have freedom *from* worry, anxiety, debt burdens, stress, and materialism; we have freedom *to* grow in generosity, in service, and in enjoying fellowship with the Lord and one another.

Financial freedom is not a destination to reach; it is a path to take. More than a checklist of things I achieve, it is a way of life. More than the peak of a mountain, it is a place where I dwell. I don't achieve "Financial Freedom" – I live in it.

We serve God and not money, meaning that money must never be a priority in making decisions. If God wants me to do something, then He will always provide the financial resources I need. God always pays for what He orders!

We must learn to master money, or money will soon master us.

When I was starting off on my career, my goal was to become financially free by the time I reached fifty. I thought that meant to accumulate a few million dollars from which I could live. In focusing on that financial goal, I became trapped in a financial swamp of wrong decisions, disloyalty, greed, dishonesty, and manipulating people. My drive to financial success came at a high price. Already at age thirty, I was a CEO traveling extensively, working long hours, and earning a lot. The price for my financial success came in three forms. My health deteriorated, and I was hospitalised for a few weeks. My relationship at home with my wife and three children was strained to the breaking point. I had no time or interest in spiritual things, and my relationship with God was almost gone. I remember sitting in church one morning thinking only of how to pay the bills the next day. So, what's the point? The goal of financial freedom in the biblical sense should never be equated to pursuing wealth, accumulating wealth, or hoarding wealth.

I was so thankful for some fellow Christian businessmen who helped me get to know what the Bible has to say about business and money. They helped me reprioritize my life and restore some balance. I started to hold on to Jesus' teaching about financial freedom. *"If you abide in my word, you are truly my disciples, and you will know the truth, and the truth will set you free"* (John 8:31-32, ESV). Financial freedom comes from living one simple truth: obedience to the Word of God sets us free. No amount of money will ever do that!

I learned that true financial freedom is independent of how much money you have. You can be financially free with lots of money. The money is not the problem. It is what you do with the money and your attitude toward it. The first church in Jerusalem solved the problem of needy believers when *"as many as were owners of lands or houses sold them and brought the proceeds of what was sold and laid it at the apostles' feet, and it was distributed to each as any had need"* (Acts 4:34-35, ESV).

Zacchaeus, a rich tax collector, met Jesus and found financial freedom. The result? He gave half his assets to the poor.

Just as you can be financially free with lots of money, you can also be in financial bondage with lots of money. We were told about the "rich, young ruler" who could not let go of his money to follow Jesus.

You can be financially free with little money. Jesus told of a poor widow who visited the Temple in Jerusalem and gave two small coins – all she had. Paul complimented the believers in Corinth when he wrote, *"in a severe test of affliction, their abundance of joy and their extreme poverty have overflowed in a wealth of generosity on their part. For they gave according to their means, as I can testify, and beyond their means, of their own accord"* (2 Corinthians 8:2-3).

There is no such thing as absolute freedom. We are only free to live and work inside defined and accepted boundaries or limitations. I am free to drive anywhere in the country – but only as long as I obey the rules of the road, keep to the speed limits, and pay my road taxes.

Financial freedom comes through obeying the "rules of the road" as set out in God's Word, rules that impose limits on spending and require me to pay my dues, both to God and Caesar!

In His Word, God gave us enough instruction to use our money well. *"All Scripture is breathed out by God and profitable for teaching, for reproof, for correction, and for training in righteousness, that the man [or woman] of God may be complete, equipped for every good work"* (2 Timothy 3:16-17, ESV).

Through the Holy Spirit, God also gave us the wisdom to make right decisions. Paul prayed for the Colossians, *". . . asking that you may be filled with the knowledge of his will in all spiritual wisdom and understanding, so as to walk in a manner worthy of the Lord, fully pleasing to him: bearing fruit in every good work . . ."* (Colossians 1:9-10, ESV).

Through Jesus, we are being empowered to manage our finances in any and every circumstance we may find ourselves, as Paul testified. *"Not that I am speaking of being in need, for I have learned in whatever situation I am to be content. I know how to be brought low, and I know how to abound. In any and every circumstance, I have learned the secret of facing plenty and hunger, abundance and need. I can do all things through him who strengthens me"* (Philippians 4:11-13, ESV).

The outcome of true financial freedom is the ability to create wealth. *"You shall remember the Lord your God, for it is he who gives you power to get wealth, that he may confirm his covenant that he swore to your fathers, as it is this day"* (Deuteronomy 8:18, ESV).

This wealth God gives us power to get is not restricted to financial wealth. Financial wealth may even be the least important aspect of wealth. The Lord will give us power to create five types of wealth.

- Spiritual wealth: the power to enjoy all privileges of being a child of God

- Physical wealth: the power to enjoy personal well-being and nice goods

- Relational wealth: the power to enjoy reciprocal relationships in love

- Productive wealth: the power to create and make things happen, improving living conditions

- Financial wealth: the power to meet our obligations, needs, and wants while being a blessing to those around us

True financial freedom brings joy

God wants us to enjoy the resources He provides. *"They celebrate your abundant goodness and joyfully sing of your righteousness"* (Psalm 145:7).

Financial freedom gives tremendous joy. There are reasons for this.

By lowering expenses below your income, you will experience far less stress and pressure. The difference between income and expenses is called margin. Margin is vitally important.

Imagine a sheet of paper without margins. It becomes unreadable as the words flow beyond the edges. Imagine your daily agenda, full of activities with no time in between. It becomes exhausting.

Our society today lives at the edge where there is no margin. Margin is the difference between stress and rest.

Without margin, we struggle, stagger, and stumble. But when margin is present, life flows. And flowing is more enjoyable than stumbling.

With margin, if your refrigerator breaks down, you don't have to break down. If your car needs servicing, you can go to the garage without wondering where the money is going to come from.

Having financial margin allows generosity toward others. This is one of the most rewarding of all human activities, an outflow of love. Meeting the needs of others delivers us from the world of selfishness and into a world of grace and gratitude. As Jesus said, *"More blessings come from giving than from receiving"* (Acts 20:35, CEV).

Four thieves of joy

Joy is a fruit of the Spirit, and you should not get robbed of your joy! Here are four thieves of joy.

1. Worry

    Having a good spending plan will help you avoid worry and anxiety. *"Therefore, I tell you, do not worry about your life, what you will eat or drink; or about your body, what you will wear. Is not life more than food, and the body more than clothes? . . . But seek first his kingdom and his righteousness, and all these things will be given to you as well"* (Matthew 6:25, 33).

2. Comparing ourselves with others

    When you compare yourself with others, you will either think you are better than others, which is pride, or think yourself worse than others, which is self-pity. Both rob you of joy. Comparison is the thief of joy and the joy of the Lord is your strength. If your joy is gone, your strength is gone.

Realizing that God gives you exactly what He knows you need at this time in your life with the responsibilities you currently have, and in line with His training program for you, you can be thankful for whatever He is giving and be joyful in that. He never makes mistakes. *"Keep your lives free from the love of money and be content with what you have, because God has said, 'Never will I leave you; never will I forsake you'"* (Hebrews 13:5).

3. Selfishness

    Giving and sharing are important elements of our spending plan. They should be visible both in our fixed costs or obligations — such as our tithe — and in our wants — such as extra giving.

    If giving is not evident, then it will lead to lack. *"One person gives freely, yet gains even more; another withholds unduly, but comes to poverty. A generous person will prosper; whoever refreshes others will be refreshed"* (Proverbs 11:24,25).

4. Discouragement

    When we are having financial problems, we can easily become discouraged. If left unchecked, it can steal our joy and hinder our ability to serve God. When you find yourself spending too much or buying the wrong things, don't get discouraged. Confess, press on, and determine not to make the same mistake again.

Sometimes we must choose to allow joy into our hearts: "I *will* rejoice!" This kind of joy is rooted in our confidence that God will answer prayer, strengthen us by His Holy Spirit, and support us through other believers. *". . . Yes, and I will continue to rejoice, for I know that through your prayers and God's provision of the Spirit of Jesus Christ what has happened to me will turn out for my deliverance"* (Philippians 1:18-19).

True financial freedom is the freedom to live, give, and grow!

—

CHAPTER 9

—

Financial Bondage

God does not want his children to be in bondage to anything. Jesus died to set you free from bondage to anything that might control you. Few areas of life have more potential for putting the believer into bondage than finances, and the sad truth is that many Christians are in financial bondage.

An old Jewish proverb says that a penny will hide the biggest star in the universe if you hold it close enough to your eye. In other words, many – including too many Christians – have become blinded by money.

This story was told by Jonathan Sacks, then Chief Rabbi in the UK. A businessman came to a rabbi asking for advice. The rabbi responded, "Look through the window. Tell me, what do you see?"

"Well, I see the world out there, trees, grass, flowers, the view is beautiful," replied the businessman.

"Now look at this mirror. What do you see?"

"I see only myself."

"That's what happens when your worldview is coated with silver; you see only yourself," replied the wise rabbi.

A focus on money alone, allowing our decisions to be based only on financial concerns, can cause us to focus only on ourselves and lead us into financial bondage.

I am so thankful for the life and ministry of Larry Burkett, a pioneer of biblical financial teaching. I traveled to the US back in 1983 to meet him and learn more about how to apply biblical principles of handling money in my life and business. Since then, I have been a student of his until his passing in 2003.

In his book, *Your Finances in Changing Times,* Burkett identified several symptoms of financial bondage that he had found common among Christians. Now, much later, these symptoms are still evident in the home, in the marketplace among businesspeople, and in all levels of our society.

These symptoms include:

1. **Overdue Bills**. We are in financial bondage when we experience anxiety from overdue bills, usually resulting from overspending splurges and "trying to keep up with the Joneses."

2. **Investment Worries**. Worrying over investments, savings, money, or assets is a cause for financial bondage and can interfere with the Christian's spiritual life.

3. **Get-Rich-Quick Attitude**. This attitude is characterized by attempts to make money quickly with very little applied effort.

4. **Deceitfulness**. We are in financial bondage if we are dishonest in financial matters. Ask yourself: Am I honest and open with everyone?

5. **Greediness**. This is a serious cause of bondage to money and the things that money can buy. Some symptoms of greed are always wanting more than we have, difficulty putting others first, inability to accept a necessary loss, always looking at what others have, and never being satisfied with what God has given us. Anyone who cannot put his own wants behind him to help satisfy the needs of others suffers from greed.

6. **Covetousness**. If we continually look at what others have and desire it, we are in financial bondage. We are also rejecting God's commandment to not envy.

7. **Unmet Family Needs**. We are in financial bondage if our family's needs cannot be met because of our buying habits, a luxurious lifestyle, or a drug habit, addiction to alcohol, gambling, etc. This can happen if we are chained with debts to the point that creditors take necessary family funds.

8. **Unmet Christian Needs**. It is the responsibility of every Christian to supply the needs of others who cannot do so for themselves. Of course, God will not lead us to meet every need of every Christian,

but we should be open to help those whom He directs us to help meet their basic needs.

9. **Over-Commitment to Work**. This is one form of financial bondage that most of us are guilty of at one time or another. A life that is devoted to business pursuits to the exclusion of all else is a life of bondage. If business or business-related activities are all we can talk about even with our family and friends, then we are experiencing some degree of financial bondage.

10. **Lack of Commitment to God's Work**. We are in financial bondage if we have no financial commitment to God's work. Basic Christian financial management can be found in Proverbs 3:9-10 and Malachi 3:10. It is only when we honor the Lord from the first part of our income that God can take control.

11. **Financial Superiority**. If we have wealth, we should not regard it primarily as a right or something owed us – even if we have honestly earned it. Instead, we should see it primarily as a responsibility: we are stewards of God's abundant riches here on earth. Read about King David's principles of stewardship in 1 Chronicles 29:10-19 to help get priorities in order.

12. **Financial Resentment.** If we do not have wealth, we may experience resentment toward God for not giving us what we feel we deserve or what we desire. Being resentful of our station in life is a form of bondage that prevents the grace and power of God from working freely and fully in our lives.

The source of all the issues on this list is pride and a focus on earthly outcomes. The antidote is humility and a focus on Christ and eternal outcomes.

The lure of materialism

Madonna sang, "I am a material girl and we're living in a material world." We all are wrapped up tightly in this material world with its accompanying philosophy of materialism.

A prevailing attitude today is "I want it and I want it now." This was illustrated perfectly by the prodigal son, who cashed in his inheritance to squander it on a selfish, indulgent lifestyle. When his money ran out and he could not meet his basic needs, he finally learned an important financial lesson: financial problems hide spiritual problems. His spiritual problems included greed, lack of discipline, ingratitude, inability to wait, discontentment, immaturity, and independence. But thankfully, there is always a way back to the Father. You can read this amazing story in Luke 15:11-32.

Materialism leads to a lack of contentment and a restless existence, always being on the move for more. A failure to answer the question, how much is enough?, leaves us open to outside forces that manipulate us to crave more.

The desire for possessions is a desire for rest. But the paradox is that we never find rest when we are possessed by the desire for more. We have become slaves to materialism, worshiping at the altar of self-indulgence and losing freedom as our possessions take control of us.

"And [Jesus] said to them, 'Take care, and be on your guard against all covetousness, for one's life does not consist in the abundance of his possessions'" (Luke 12:15).

Materialism is nothing less than idolatry — perhaps the sin mentioned most often in the Bible. Although idolatry is described in different ways, it usually involves putting something else in the place of God, often something that humans have made themselves. In a typical reference, Isaiah writes, *". . . They bow down to the work of their hands, to what their own fingers have made"* (Isaiah 2:8). In the New Testament, the apostle Paul repeatedly condemns idolatry, criticizing those who *"exchanged the glory of the immortal God for images made to look like a mortal human being . . ."* (Romans 1: 23).

Materialism is defined as "the preoccupation with material things rather than intellectual or spiritual things." It is wrong for a Christian to be preoccupied with material things. That is not to say we can't have material things, but the obsession with acquiring and caring for "stuff" is a dangerous thing for the disciple of Jesus. More and more, we worship at the altar of materialism that feeds our egos through the acquisition of more stuff. Our homes are filled with all manner of possessions. We build bigger and bigger houses with more cupboards and storage space to house all the things we buy – even worse when our buying incurs debt.

Our insatiable desire for more, better, and newer stuff is nothing more than covetousness. The tenth commandment tells us not to fall victim to coveting. God wants more for us than just to rein in our buying sprees. He knows we will never be happy indulging our materialistic desires when they are a trap of the enemy to keep our focus on ourselves rather than on God.

What do you think about when you first wake up? What's on your mind just before you fall asleep? If your first and last thoughts of the day are centered on money – earning more, saving more, spending more, or paying off more – money and possessions may be an idol to you.

The Bible tells us to control our own thoughts, to *"take captive every thought to make it obedient to Christ"* (2 Corinthians 10:5).

Financial idolatry is real, and it's alive and well in the world today. Recognizing it is half the battle as well as the first step toward rooting it out.

"While Paul was . . . in Athens, he was greatly distressed to see that the city was full of idols" (Acts 17:16). He was spiritually disturbed. Unless we feel – we sense and experience – distress, uneasiness, and spiritual discomfort, all talk about idols will be meaningless.

"Stuffocation"

"Stuffocation" is a new word that we could easily add to our dictionary. The trend watcher James Wallmann coined the term to describe the feeling that too many things, too much stuff, is suffocating our way of life. Thanks to mass production and global markets, we have access to a huge amount of relatively cheap products that we readily buy — and then store! The explosion of self-storage facilities over the past ten years testifies to the fact that we have too much stuff and too little space to keep it. Not only too little physical space but also too little emotional space. The excess of stuff is beginning to show us that more is, in fact, less.

We have reached a clutter crisis. The more we have, the more stress it brings. It all has to be managed, used, repaired, stored, and maintained — more worries and less satisfaction than we expected.

So, what is the antidote for our stuffocation?

My suggestion is to start giving stuff away. Jesus Himself said, *"It is more blessed to give than to receive."* Join in the "sharing economy" in which cars, mowers, tools, and even money can be shared with family and neighbors.

Downsizing your stuff can bring extra space in which to breathe. In the end, our life does not depend on how much stuff we can gather. The well-known bumper sticker "He who dies with the most toys wins" just doesn't ring true.

Jesus told of a rich man who wanted to enjoy life by living off his accumulated assets. *". . . Take care, and be on your guard against all covetousness, for one's life does not consist in the abundance of his possessions"* (Luke 12:15, ESV).

"And he told them a parable, saying, 'The land of a rich man produced plentifully, and he thought to himself, "What shall I do, for I have nowhere to store my crops?" And he said, "I will do this: I will tear down my barns and build larger ones, and there I will store all my grain and my goods. And I will say to my soul, 'Soul, you have ample goods laid up for many years; relax, eat, drink, be merry.'" But God said to him, "Fool! This night your soul is required of you, and the things you have prepared, whose will they be?" So is the one who lays up treasure for himself and is not rich toward God'" (Luke 12:16-21, ESV).

Financial bondage resulting from materialism and stuffocation can end in catastrophe, as just told in the parable of the rich man. God expects more from us – to be selfless with the financial resources He's blessed us with, not selfish. This week think about some stuff you have that you could give away. Who could you make happy with it?

—

CHAPTER 10

—

Decisions

When traveling the path of financial discipleship with the Lord, stages along the way require major decisions that will affect our discipleship. The ultimate stage is to work in such a way that the Master will be able to say, *"Well done, good and faithful servant . . . Enter into the joy of your master"* (Matthew 25:21, ESV). That should be the goal of the financial disciple.

These stages are represented here as a hierarchy. You cannot reach the second level without first making your decision about the first.

But these stages are not simply linear; they are also circular. Life brings ups and downs, successes and failures. This means going back to where you started and revisiting your decisions to see whether you are still adhering to them in practice. Decisions you need to revisit include "one-time" important decisions as well as daily choices that are part of life's challenges and setbacks. These decisions form a trail of guideposts along your journey, pointing you back to that time when you decided to follow Jesus as a disciple. They encourage you to carry on in the midst of life's problems.

1. Salvation Decision – "I trust Him for salvation."

This is God's free gift to all mankind as a result in accepting Christ's work of redemption on the cross. It is the starting point for becoming children of God. *"But to all who did receive him, who believed in his name, he gave the right to become children of God"* (John 1:12, ESV).

As children of God and financial disciples, we can build our lives on this salvation: salvation from the penalty of sin because Christ has paid the price; salvation from the power of sin because He lives in us and empowers us through His Spirit to live for Him.

2. Lordship Decision – "He will have control of my life."

Lordship is both a one-time surrender and a daily transformation as we allow Jesus to lead us and we follow His ways. We will ask the question, "What would Jesus do?" to guide us as we make life's important decisions.

The Lord's ways are so very different from our ways, and the way He thinks is so different from the way we think. If we want the best for our lives, we will ask the Lord to reveal His thoughts and help us follow His ways. *"For my thoughts are not your thoughts, neither are your ways my ways, declares the Lord. For as the heavens are higher than the earth, so are my ways higher than your ways and my thoughts than your thoughts"* (Isaiah 55:8-9, ESV).

3. Calling Decision — "I am called to use gifts, talents, experiences, and opportunities exactly where I am for God's glory."

Everyone has a calling consisting of specific works that God has for you. Paul wrote, *"With this in mind, we constantly pray for you, that our God may make you worthy of his calling, and that by his power he may bring to fruition your every desire for goodness and your every deed prompted by faith"* (2 Thessalonians 1:11).

4. Stewardship Decision — "As a steward, I am responsible for managing everything God has entrusted to me for His glory."

God calls us to be faithful with the management of all He has given us, and we will be held accountable for how we use His resources. Jesus gave us the principle when He talked to His disciples about the coming of the Kingdom of Heaven. *"Again, it will be like a man going on a journey, who called his servants and entrusted his wealth to them"* (Matthew 25:14).

Therefore, we should strive to be trustworthy stewards so that we will be found faithful when we are held accountable by the Lord. *"Moreover, it is required of stewards that they be found faithful. But with me it is a very small thing that I should be judged by you or by any human court. In fact, I do not even judge myself. For I am not aware of anything against myself, but I am not thereby acquitted. It is the Lord who judges me"* (1 Corinthians 4:2-4, ESV).

5. Treasure Decision — "I am to be a pipeline of God's grace financially, relationally, spiritually, etc."

Treasure that is transferred to the Kingdom has the power to accomplish Kingdom work and to change the heart of the giver. Paul wrote to his disciple, Timothy, *"Command them [the rich] to do good, to be rich in good deeds, and to be generous and willing to share. In this way they will lay up treasure for themselves as a firm foundation for the coming age, so that they may take hold of the life that is truly life"* (1 Timothy 6:18-19).

6. Discipleship Decision – "I will be committed to disciple others."

In the Great Commission, Jesus commands us to *"go and make disciples,"* and to *"teach these new disciples to obey all the commands I have given you"* (Matthew 28:19-20, NLT). If Jesus was being literal, then all means ALL, including both discipleship and His teachings on money and possessions. Embracing our responsibility as financial disciples means committing to learn, apply, and teach biblical financial principles. It also means to accompany people in helping them grow in intimacy with Jesus, teaching them to obey all He has commanded. Discipleship is *the* way Christ gives us to multiply His kingdom.

Have you made these decisions? Are you staying with these decisions?

The path of financial discipleship – from stuck to servant

As we listen to Jesus while traveling the path of discipleship, He is helping us in our finances to move from what could be called "stuck" through "struggling" to "stable" to "solid" and then to "servanthood." This is also a path we can tread to help others become the *"good and faithful servant"* the Lord is looking for.

1. Stuck

This is the state of being financially unhealthy and often in denial that anything is wrong in our financial life. In this stage, people are not open to change; they deny reality and run from help with their life in turmoil.

Stuck people need loving confrontation to see their need for change. Some tough love is required here, challenging them to get serious and improve their finances. *"As iron sharpens iron, so one person sharpens another"* (Proverbs 27:17). Sometimes sparks need to fly!

2. Struggling

People struggling with their finances realize that they are not in a good way; they want to change and are ready to receive help.

In this stage, people need practical, interesting, and common-sense teaching. When navigating finances, godly counsel is essential. *"Two are better than one, because they have a good return for their labor: if either of them falls down, one can help the other up. But pity anyone who falls and has no one to help them up"* (Ecclesiastes 4:9-10).

3. Stable

People with stable finances are generally financially healthy. They have visible financial success and show increased confidence, but they may still be self-focused. Learning to grow in Christ-centered generosity will help to avoid being self-centered.

In this stage, people need biblical teaching blended with practical truth.

4. Solid

Those who have become financially solid are learning from Scripture, motivated to follow biblical principles, and want to apply what God has to say about handling money and possessions. They may need to learn to give sacrificially and to plan their finances with God, setting faith goals that reflect His will for their lives.

In this stage, people need to go deeper into God's Word and apply the truths found there.

5. Servant

Financial disciples are servants to God and their neighbors, modeling financial faithfulness. They are generous, investing their time, treasure, and talents in Kingdom work. They are eager to pass on to others what they have learned.

Servants need to learn to "deny self," follow Jesus, and make financial disciples.

Developing a servant mindset

Modern personal-finance teaching tends to reside somewhere between spending and saving, while failing to recognise a third important dimension: servanthood. Our culture views the accumulation of wealth as an all-important and laudable activity. Capitalism is built upon the central drive within the human heart to acquire more and more. Most people who view themselves as mature when it comes to money are savers, proud of their achievements in building wealth.

Our aim as financial disciples is to be servants. Paul expresses a penetrating description of serving God as a faithful servant, *"This is how one should regard us, as servants of Christ and stewards of the mysteries of God. Moreover, it is required of stewards that they be found faithful"* (1 Corinthians 4:1-2, ESV).

The word Paul uses for "servants"' is the Greek "*hupereeretas,*" which is used for under-rowers in a Roman galley. The masters up on top determine the direction, pace, and leadership, while the captives on the benches down under do all the hard work, rowing the boat to a constant drumbeat. A faithful steward is therefore an "under rower": someone totally submitted to the master; under his direction, pace, and leadership; willing to pull on the oars and work hard. Sometimes we must, as "under rowers" in the lower reaches of a kind of Roman galley, be willing to accept everything the world above us throws on our head. That is our assignment: to serve no matter what the cost.

Along the path of financial discipleship, we can recognize three major milestones: spender, saver, and servant. Your money mindset is driven by two factors: your temporal focus and your view on the highest purpose of money. Spenders maximize value today; savers maximize value in the future; servants maximize value in eternity.

- **Spenders,** represented by most people in the Western world, commonly pursue the greatest possible present consumption, even if mindful of the need to save. Spenders view financial resources as a way to live it up, enjoying every part of the high life that money can buy.

- **Savers,** by contrast, strive to limit consumption to some extent, focusing instead on increased wealth accumulation. Savers have a more complex view of money, seeing it mostly as a tool for security, stability, flexibility, and personal freedom.

- **Servants,** possessing the rarest mindset of all, orient their life around limiting both consumption and wealth-building, focusing instead on giving the most money they can toward blessing other people. Servants view their money as a potential blessing to the world in Christ's name, desiring to make the most of its potential for positive impact.

How do you tell which money mindset you have?

Ask yourself, "Where would I focus my thoughts and efforts if my income began to increase dramatically over time?" If you would spend, spend, and spend some more to enjoy all the world has to offer, you are – you guessed it – a spender.

If you would seek to pay off the mortgage early, retire early, or build a family dynasty of wealth, you may be a saver.

If you would immediately begin thinking about how to give your excess resources to Christian initiatives around the world, you're definitely a servant.

Those with a servant's attitude have changed their spending and saving priorities.

Their spending decisions will be made on the basis that God owns everything and that they, as responsible stewards, will look upon spending as investing in a present lifestyle that reflects God's principles. It will be prayerful, responsible, and focused on enough rather than more.

Saving and investing decisions will be made by prayerfully determining God-given goals for their financial future as they limit spending to achieve these goals. Investing for eternal impact in the Kingdom of God is a priority.

Servants make decisions that grow their Kingdom account, build their eternal net worth, and generate an eternal return on their investments.

—

CHAPTER 11

—

Financial Success

Ron Blue, founder of Kingdom Advisors, tells of the time when he was asked to testify to a senate sub-committee about family finances.

The question from Senator Dodd of Connecticut was, "What advice about money would you give the American family?"

I swallowed hard, knowing my answer was going to sound overly simple to him. "Well, Senator, I would tell them four things. Spend less than you earn, avoid debt, save for the unexpected, and set long-term goals."

The senator picked up his pencil and asked me to repeat myself. I did.

Looking down at me over his glasses, he said, "It seems that would work at any income level."

By now I was gaining my footing. I decided to take my chances. "Yes, sir, even for the United States government!"

Spending less than you earn is the simple way to financial prosperity. Although it sounds easy, it is difficult for many to maintain. It means developing a plan for spending, making sure that there is a surplus each month, and keeping to the plan. This builds a cash reserve to see us through emergencies and provide for future needs.

Avoiding debt will keep us out of trouble and ensure we have first priority on how we spend our money. Debt drains our resources and can cause us to lose our freedom as we become a *"slave to the lender"* (Proverbs 22:7).

Saving for the unexpected enables us to have enough reserves to meet emergencies without going into debt. People and companies who flourish through troubling times are those who maintain cash reserves.

Setting long-term goals together with our spouse and the Lord in prayer helps us quantify God's will for us. It motivates us to save and invest for the future. Above all, we should set goals for eternity and build up an "eternity portfolio" of treasures in heaven.

Ron Blue later added a fifth and a sixth principle to his initial four. The fifth principle is to give generously, because giving breaks the power of money over us. It is an act of worship, acknowledging that all we have comes from God. Out of this came the sixth principle: "Believe God owns it all and live by it!" That will see us through any danger, trouble, or faltering economy.

When all else fails – the Lord never fails. Sometimes, for good reasons beyond our comprehension, the Lord withholds from us. He may even remove our hedge of protection as He did with Job. If we are wise in such times, we will fall back on God Himself and trust Him for the outcome, which will always ultimately be to our benefit.

Spending plan – the practical application of financial principles

Here are six reasons why a spending plan, or budget, makes sense.

First, a spending plan reduces conflict in marriage. It provides built-in accountability and an objective standard for all of your spending decisions. A couple can easily make 1500 to 2000 transactions each year. With no spending plan to allocate your income to reflect your priorities, any of these expenditures could set off an argument.

Second, a spending plan makes you create and maintain a vision for the future. It provides the guidelines you need to successfully spend less than you earn, which is the key to long-term financial security.

If you want to buy a home, start your own business, fund your children's education, or plan for your retirement, a spending plan can keep you focused on your goals.

Third, a spending plan brings unity into a marriage. It enables you to make objective and impartial decisions based on common criteria. When your budget is drafted with input from both spouses, spending and saving decisions are not "mine or yours, but ours."

Fourth, a spending plan helps couples communicate. You cannot establish a budget without talking about priorities, needs, goals, and dreams. Discussing how and on what basis you make decisions increases your understanding of how each unique personality contributes to the partnership.

Fifth, establishing a spending plan sets a great example for your children. When they see your financial discipline and how you are making progress toward reaching your goals, they learn valuable lessons on how to handle their money.

Last and most important, a spending plan is a practical expression of God's ownership. You are not planning to spend your money, but God's money, and this brings an extra dimension of responsibility to the table.

Six decisions to make

Decision 1: Acknowledge Gods ownership and priority.

"Honor the Lord with your wealth, with the first fruits of all your crops; then your barns will be filled to overflowing, and your vats will brim over with new wine" (Proverbs 3:9-10).

You honor the Lord's ownership and provision when you honor Him with your money. This means prayerfully making a spending plan by which you agree with God about how you are to utilize His money. It means to give the Lord His part first.

Decision 2: Spend less than you earn.

Develop a spending plan made of three parts. (1) Obligations: fixed costs like mortgage, rent, insurances, subscriptions etc. (2) Needs: variable costs such as supermarket, clothes, cosmetics, toiletries, etc. (3) Wants: things we want to buy. This includes saving for emergencies like car repairs, new household appliances, etc. It also includes vacations, home improvements, a new car, and even long-term investments.

Don't live on the edge; develop a margin between income and expenses. To create your financial future, you need savings – investing for future wants. A lot of spending plans fail to include saving for future wants, including reserves for emergencies. This is no way to plan for the future.

Decision 3: Avoid debt.

When you are spending all you have on obligations and needs, you have to supplement your income with borrowing. This reduces your opportunity to serve in the future and risks getting into even more debt. The very best financial decision of all is to pay off debts. No other financial choice gives better results, not only financially but also in peace of mind and freedom.

"Live within your harvest," accepting what you have and making do with it. More than a strategy, this is a conviction, the kind where you drive a stake and declare it so.

Living within your harvest is possible – it just isn't popular. It conveys that you have boundaries and that you are willing to *confine* yourself within the scope of these boundaries rather than yearn for the alleged greener grass on the other side of the fence.

Contentment and simplicity are invaluable friends in this effort, as we will see in the next chapters. Content yourself with what God sends your way and live a simple life of righteousness. Then God, honored by your devotion, will care for both your margin and your harvest.

Decision 4: Increase margin.

There are three ways to increase your financial margin: decrease spending, increase income, or increase savings. Among these choices, the easiest is to simply reduce spending. It sounds easy, but as we all know from experience, it's hard to sustain. The context of our culture screams against restraint, and every message we receive – from ads in every form of media to our neighbor's new van – all urge us to cave in.

It is healthy to periodically separate from the things of the world and do without. In traditional thinking, such fasting pertains to food. But in the context of financial margin, it is good to fast from shopping for periods of time. Use up what you have in the refrigerator and freezer. Wear out whatever clothes you have in the closet. Get along on whatever you have in the house. Remember the cloth poster on Grandma's kitchen wall? "Use it up. Wear it out. Make it do. Do without."

The world does not stop, nor does the family fall apart when we unplug from the treadmill of consumerism for a period. About the only momentous thing that will happen is your finances will be resuscitated by a much-needed transfusion of margin.

Paying off debts can lead to the ability to increase savings. Making payments on loans is like filling a bath with no plug. Your income drains away. Plugging the hole by becoming debt-free releases margin you can put toward achieving your long-term goals.

Decision 5: Give generously.

You are never more like Jesus than when you are giving. He is a giver, and you can never out-give God. Giving breaks the power of money as you transfer money into the Kingdom economy. It opens a window through which God can pour out blessings on your life.

Decision 6: Set long-term goals.

Sit down together with God. In prayer by faith ask Him to reveal His goals for your life. Then ask what finances these goals will need. Set a faith goal, which is a statement like: "I believe God is leading me to _____." When He has revealed this to you, you need to internalize it, believing it with your whole heart. Faith goals give direction and purpose, helping you to crystalize your thinking and planning.

Such goals provide personal motivation, and you can trust God to direct your steps.

If your faith goals are made together with God, He will provide. God always pays for what He orders. If the Lord puts something on my heart to do, I have learned never to say, "I cannot afford it." Such a response is faithless. Whether it concerns leaving a well-paid job to take on an assignment in the Kingdom, participating in a conference overseas, or making a special donation when it is needed, I have always seen God's faithful provision.

Regularly evaluating my finances according to these decisions has led to financial growth. However, there is a downside to focusing on financial success.

The problem with financial success

Ron Blue says, "Financial success is really so simple. Spend less that you earn over a long period of time, and you will be successful." However, there is a significant problem with financial success.

A documentary on Dutch TV described the rise to fame of a Dutch artist Folkert de Jong, one of the most successful contemporary artists in Holland. His expressive sculptures and installations sell like hot cakes. Rich collectors, like Charles Saatchi, Damien First, and Tracey Emin fought each other for his work.

Folkert de Jong told of his journey. "One minute you are making something in your atelier in old Amsterdam and the next it's worth forty thousand euros or even a hundred thousand." His ever-increasing bank balance sent him crazy, he tells. "All of a sudden there were assistants and other office workers, and it became much more commercial. I held lots of exhibitions and had to produce more and more. It was like becoming another person, driven by money and power."

Eventually stress tore him apart as he constantly argued with his business friends, who "turned out not to be friends at all." This all led to bankruptcy and left him with a debt of over half a million euros.

"I knew I had to get back to basics, back to myself," Folkert said. "I made by best work when I had no prospects at all!"

People around the world would generally agree that having money is more fun than not having any. It seems logical, but is it always true? Does having more money always bring joy and fulfillment?

I find managing money to be a big challenge, no matter if I have a lot or a little. There are always many people wanting it – government, suppliers, even friends and family.

This mirrors the experience of probably the richest man who ever lived, King Solomon. He said, *"Those who love money will never have enough. How meaningless to think that wealth brings true happiness!*

The more you have, the more people come to help you spend it. So what good is wealth – except perhaps to watch it slip through your fingers! People who work hard sleep well, whether they eat little or much. But the rich seldom get a good night's sleep"
(Ecclesiastes 5:10-12, NLT).

Our new washing machine was delivered this week. We bought it online at CoolBlue. This store has known explosive growth and is now a huge online retailer. Started in 1999 by three students, CoolBlue now has sales of over one-and-a-half billion euros! The CEO, Pieter Zwart, was interviewed (wearing a cool blue shirt) and was asked, "What does money mean to you?" His reply was insightful. "I thought that life would be more interesting with money than without. Well, that's partly true. It's just that the law of diminishing returns comes into play. Once you have reached a certain level, it is no longer important how much more money you have. It is so difficult to turn money into enjoyment! To be happy and have money do not necessarily go together."

So, what could you do in the middle of all this competition for your money? Well, first give thanks to God that you have some money to buy necessities for your family and that you can help sustain the government through taxes.

Look at your spending plan again. Are there ways to cut down on spending, so that you can increase savings or giving?

He who dies with the most toys wins?

On TV, I watched the US president visiting the house where Mahatma Gandhi had lived in Delhi. It reminded me of my own visit to Delhi – and the startling contrast with a bumper sticker I had seen years earlier: "He who dies with the most toys wins."

When Gandhi died, he had less than ten possessions, including a watch, spectacles, sandals, and an eating bowl. He was a man of non-possession and didn't even own his own home. He practiced simplicity and minimalism in all areas of his life, leaving behind a huge legacy in how to live a life of simplicity. Gandhi believed in possessing little except the clothes he wore and some utensils for cooking and eating. He used to give away or auction any gifts given to him.

The brief list of possessions Gandhi had when he died proves that his worth was surely not measured in what he owned. Not that he was against having good material things. He said, "You may have occasion to possess or use material things, but the secret of life lies in never missing them." Just how attached are we to material things?

It seems that we are still right in the middle of growth-fueled, unbridled consumerism. Accumulating possessions still seems to be the measure of our achievements, as if our net worth determines our self-worth.

Gandhi did not condemn wealth. Rather, he condemned attachment to it, the prison of being possessed by possessions. He said, "If one has wealth, it does not mean that it should be thrown away and wife and children should be turned out of doors. It simply means that one must give up attachment of these things!"

My good friend Dr. Andrés Panasiuk says, "We need to cut the emotional umbilical cord that attaches us to our possessions."

We spend a lot of money, time, and energy looking after our possessions. By having fewer things to possess and look after, our life naturally becomes simpler. I believe this contributes to a good life of contentment and thankfulness for what we have.

Richard Foster, author of the great book, *The Freedom of Simplicity*, stated (simply of course) that "Simplicity is freedom."

Simplicity is an inward reality that results in an outward lifestyle. The inward reality of simplicity is beautifully encapsulated in Jesus' message in Matthew 6 that we are to seek first the kingdom of God and the righteousness of this kingdom, and then all that is needed for life will be added to us.

Foster writes, "Three key attitudes of heart help to summarize this internal focus. If what we have we can receive as a gift from God; and if what we have is to be used for God; and if what we have can be available to others when it is clearly right and good, then we are living in the inward reality of simplicity."

With apologies to René Descartes, *"Consumo Ego Sum,"* or "I spend, therefore I am" seems to be the modern, guiding answer to our search for identity. But our worth and meaning should never be found in what we possess.

Keith & Kristyn Getty are probably my favorite Christian musicians, and one of my favorite songs is, "My Worth Is Not in What I Own."

> My worth is not in what I own
> Not in the strength of flesh and bone
> But in the costly wounds of love
> At the cross
>
> My worth is not in skill or name
> In win or lose, in pride or shame
> But in the blood of Christ that flowed
> At the cross
>
> I rejoice in my Redeemer
> Greatest Treasure
> Wellspring of my soul
> I will trust in Him, no other
> My soul is satisfied in Him alone
>
> As summer flowers we fade and die
> Fame, youth and beauty hurry by
> But life eternal calls to us
> At the cross
>
> I will not boast in wealth or might

Or human wisdom's fleeting light
But I will boast in knowing Christ
At the cross

Two wonders here that I confess
My worth and my unworthiness
My value fixed – my ransom paid
At the cross

PART 2: WHAT IS "FINANCIAL" DISCIPLESHIP?

—

CHAPTER 12

—

Eternal Perspective

Jesus said, *"Do not store up for yourselves treasures on earth, where moths and vermin destroy, and where thieves break in and steal. But store up for yourselves treasures in heaven, where moths and vermin do not destroy, and where thieves do not break in and steal. For where your treasure is, there your heart will be also"* (Matthew 6:19-21).

It's not really about treasure, it's about our heart. All of life is a treasure hunt for a perfect person and a perfect place. Meeting this perfect person and reaching the perfect place has everything to do with our heart's priorities.

Why not treasures on earth? First, it's just a poor investment, and second, Jesus says that they capture the human spirit. The things of the world tend to bind us to the world, where thieves come in and vermin destroy.

Jesus went on to say that where your treasure is, your heart will also be. So, if we are focused on building treasures on earth, those earthly treasures can capture our human spirit and take us away from God. Jesus described the futility of storing up treasures on earth, saying that "moths and vermin" would destroy them. Jesus was warning about risks like inflation, market changes or devaluation that can consume our investments. Circumstances change. We lose our jobs. The things upon which we have built our lives can slowly crumble away. They can also vanish in a heartbeat.

Thieves can break in and steal. We have to deal with corruption, extortion, greed, and deception from people who steal from us. Even something inanimate like debt can steal our freedom. Our fear of loss drives us to protect and preserve what we have, leading to yet another theft – our joy. Focusing on earthly treasures is just a poor investment.

We are created for something higher and much more worthwhile. We should be devoted to God and His plans for us because the Kingdom is our inheritance. Esau, one of the sons of Jacob, sold his whole inheritance for a single meal; sometimes we sell a whole inheritance in the Kingdom of God for temporary treasures. Possessions and the things of the world capture our heart, drawing our attention and focus away from eternal things to imprison them in the land of the unworthy.

The location of your treasures can be determined by answering these questions. What do you value most? If the things you value most are material things, then you are focused on worldly, temporal treasures. What do you think of most? What is consuming your time?

I remember my first portfolio of shares in the stock market. I invested something like 20,000 euros during the summer of 2001. I remember watching the share prices several times a day. I knew it was really capturing my thinking. Well, we know what happened on the 11th of September that year. We had a major financial crash and the price of my shares went through the floor.

It took, I think, eight years for those share prices to come back to something approaching their original level. But for all that time, I confess that my attention was captured.

What would you most hate to lose? If your focus is on things that you would hate to lose, then you're thinking about treasures on earth. But remember, "whatever I keep, I will sooner or later, lose." Some things will fall out of fashion; others will need replacing. Everything on earth is transient – it was created to be. The Lord's primary concern is with our focus. He wants us to keep our focus on his values – superior and eternal – as *they* were created to be. Unfortunately, treasures on earth are a battleground for our hearts.

Being focused on earthly treasures is a violation of the first commandment, which is idolatry. But the more our vision locks on to eternity, on treasures in heaven, the less we will focus on treasures on earth.

It is interesting to read that Jesus said, "Store up *for yourselves* treasures in heaven." While I believe Jesus is more concerned with our heart than our treasure, He does want us to build up a store of "treasure in heaven" for our own use.

What are these treasures in heaven? I believe that the greatest treasure in heaven is an intimate relationship with Jesus Christ and the anticipation of hearing *"Well done, good and faithful servant. Enter into the joy of your master"* (Matthew 25:21, ESV).

Second, we are promised positions of authority. The Bible says we will reign with Christ as kings, as it were, in the new heaven and the new earth when God will recreate this earth to be something perfect. We will find this perfect person to have this intimate relationship with, and we will find the perfect place in which we can reign and have authority as leaders in this new earth God has promised.

There are five heavenly crowns mentioned in the New Testament that will be awarded to believers. They are the imperishable crown, the crown of rejoicing, the crown of righteousness, the crown of glory, and the crown of life. The Greek word for "crown" is *"stephanos"* (the source for the name Stephen, the martyr) and means "a badge of royalty, a prize in the public games or a symbol of honor." Used during the ancient Greek games, it referred to a wreath or garland of leaves placed on a victor's head as a reward for winning an athletic contest. As such, this word is used figuratively in the New Testament of the heavenly rewards that God promises to those who are faithful.

The Bible talks about "hidden manna" to sustain us all the time. Then in the new Temple and the new Jerusalem, we will be able to eat from the tree of life in paradise. We will receive praise from the angels. We will be given white robes, a white stone, and a new name. We will be given a new home – the new city, the heavenly Jerusalem – where justice and peace will reign and where there is provision for all.

We will experience this perfect place in eternity. Isn't that a great thing for the disciple to look forward to?

Developing our treasures in heaven

Paul was grateful to the believers in Philippi for their financial support. *"Not that I desire your gifts; what I desire is that more be credited to your account"* (Philippians 4:17). Financial generosity will result in a credit to our heavenly account.

In fact, Jesus indicated that the measure in which we will build up our treasures in heaven will be determined by the measure in which we share. *"Give, and it will be given to you. A good measure, pressed down, shaken together and running over, will be poured into your lap. For with the measure you use, it will be measured to you"* (Luke 6:38).

Jesus' counsel to the rich, young ruler who wanted to know how to inherit eternal life was radical. *"Sell all that you have and distribute to the poor, and you will have treasure in heaven; and come, follow me"* (Luke 18:22, ESV). Giving to the poor will build treasures in heaven.

Rather than building up riches for ourselves, doing good and sharing will increase our eternal capital. *"As for the rich in this present age, charge them not to be haughty, nor to set their hopes on the uncertainty of riches, but on God, who richly provides us with everything to enjoy. They are to do good, to be rich in good works, to be generous and ready to share, thus storing up treasure for themselves as a good foundation for the future, so that they may take hold of that which is truly life"* (1 Timothy 6:17-19, ESV).

—

CHAPTER 13

—

Learning from the Master

Jesus' parables were stories to illustrate a truth, teaching aids that can be thought of as extended analogies or inspired comparisons. A common description of a parable is that it is an earthly story with a heavenly meaning. As Jesus and his disciples walked together and experienced life, Jesus often used what they saw and heard to teach them about money and possessions.

Jesus' kind of teaching was far more effective than what we get in a normal classroom. Research has shown that learning from classroom lectures accounts for ten percent of what we really absorb. Mentoring or coaching accounts for twenty percent. The remaining seventy percent – the vast majority – comes from the kind of hands-on experience Jesus gave his disciples.

Here is a brief overview of how Jesus used financial or economic situations to teach important lessons.

1. Jesus referred to investment in jewels and treasures to illustrate the importance of investing in the Kingdom of God (the parables of the treasure hidden in the field and the valuable pearl: Matthew 13:44-46).

2. He referred to saving new treasures as well as old treasures to illustrate the importance of storing up both new and old truths (the parable of the owner of a house and his treasures, new and old: Matthew 13:52).

3. He used indebtedness to illustrate the importance of forgiveness (the parable of the unmerciful servant: Matthew 18:23-30).

4. He referred to hiring procedures and wage structures to illustrate God's sovereignty and generosity in treating all with equality, forgiving sins, and rewarding people with eternal life (the parable of the workers in the vineyard: Matthew 20:1-16).

5. He told a story of a fruit farmer who leased his property to illustrate the way the chief priests and Pharisees were rejecting the Son of God (the parable of the tenants: Matthew 21:33-43).

6. He discussed capital, investments, banking, and interest to emphasize our human responsibility to utilize God's gifts in a prudent and responsible way (the parable of the talents: Matthew 25:14-30; the parable of the ten minas: Luke 19:11-27).

7. He referred to money lenders, interest, and debt cancelation to illustrate the importance of love and appreciation to God for canceling our debt of sin (Luke 7:41-43).

8. He spoke of building barns to store grain for the future while neglecting to store up spiritual treasures as a very foolish decision (the parable of the rich fool: Luke 12:16-21).

9. He used architectural planning, building construction, and cost analysis to illustrate the importance of future planning and counting the cost before we make decisions in building our spiritual lives (Luke 14:28-30).

10. He used the human joy that comes from finding lost money to illustrate the joy in the presence of angels when a lost soul believes in Christ (Luke 15:8-10).

11. He used wealth, dividing up the estate, irresponsible spending, and a change of heart to illustrate repentance and forgiveness (the parable of the prodigal son: Luke 15:11-32).

12. He used bad financial management and dishonest debt reduction to illustrate that sometimes people are wiser in their worldly realm than honest followers of Christ are in the spiritual realm (the parable of the shrewd manager: Luke 16:1-12).

13. He told of a rich man who died and went to hell, contrasting him with a poor beggar who died and went to heaven. This was to illustrate how wealth and its benefits may harden our hearts against spiritual truth (the parable of the rich man and Lazarus: Luke 16:19-31).

14. He contrasted the proud Pharisee who fasted and tithed regularly, with the humble tax collector who acknowledged the sin of

dishonesty and greed. This was to illustrate that God acknowledges humility and rejects self-exaltation (the parable of the Pharisee and tax collector: Luke 18:9-14).

15. He used a ripe grain field and harvesters to illustrate "spiritually ripe hearts" in Samaria, and the part the apostles would have in harvesting people's souls (John 4:34-38).

In the coming chapters, we will look at some stories Jesus used to explain how to deal with money and possessions in a little more detail.

PART 3: LEARNING FROM THE MASTER

—

CHAPTER 14

—

The Debtors

Read Luke 7:36-50.

Core text

"'Two people owed money to a certain moneylender. One owed him five hundred denarii, and the other fifty. Neither of them had the money to pay him back, so he forgave the debts of both. Now which of them will love him more?' Simon replied, 'I suppose the one who had the bigger debt forgiven.' 'You have judged correctly,' Jesus said."

Jesus used a lot of examples from daily life to illustrate important principles. A denarius was a silver coin that was the equivalent of a day's wages.

In the parable of the two debtors, Simon, a Pharisee, has invited Jesus to a dinner at his house.

A woman appears at the dinner table, which would have been set up in a courtyard. This location, along with an open gate, was commonly used to enable the rest of the town to look in on the festivities. The woman is described by Luke as a "sinner." She goes specifically to see Jesus, having brought an expensive alabaster jar of perfume to anoint Him.

She anoints His feet with perfume, she weeps and wets them with tears, and she kisses them repeatedly. Kissing Jesus' feet was a public sign of deep humility, devotion, and gratitude.

The dinner guests are shocked by this display, objecting to it on many levels. A woman letting her hair down is an intimate gesture which would never be done in front of anyone other than her husband. According to some rabbinical writings, if a woman let her hair down in public, it was considered grounds for divorce. And here is an immoral woman doing that very thing at a dinner table full of men. To make matters worse, she is touching a man who is not a relative; this is something that no moral woman would do. Simon and his dinner guests judge this to be completely unacceptable.

Jesus then refers to two debtors, one forgiven 50 denarii (about six weeks' wages) and another, 500 denarii (one-and-one-half years' wages). The moneylender forgave them both. Now, Jesus asks simply, which debtor would be more grateful? Simon must make a judgment.

Jesus agrees with Simon's conclusion but then takes the conversation in an unexpected direction. He says that the woman — judged to be a sinner — has acted more graciously than Simon — judged to be a righteous man. Jesus then announces that *"Her many sins have been forgiven — as her great love has shown"* (Luke 7:47).

It is important to understand that she was not forgiven because of her deeds, because Jesus then added, *"Your faith has saved you; go in peace"* (Luke 7:50).

Do you relate more to the religious leader, Simon, or to the sinful woman? The good news of this parable is that sinners can find forgiveness through faith in Jesus. There is no one who is too far gone, too sinful, too bad. All it takes is to go to Jesus in faith. May we be more like Jesus, who accepts all who come to him in faith.

Contrast also how Simon and the woman spent their money. Simon held a lavish feast — with Jesus as the main event — to impress all of his friends. The widow sacrificed money to worship Jesus out of a heart full of remorse and worship.

In both the Old and New Testaments, the phrases "cancel a debt," "forgive a debt," and "forgive a sin" are often expressed with the same words. In this case, the verb used for canceling the debt has its root in the Greek word *"charis,"* which is often translated as grace. Throughout the New Testament, the verb "to forgive" is used both as a financial term, as in forgiving a debt, and as a religious term, as in forgiving sins. Jesus was speaking of financial debt in the parable, but as we will see, the creditor/debtor language is also used in reference to God and His forgiveness of sin.

Jesus is also teaching His disciples about the forgiveness of financial debt. This appeals to the hopelessness of satisfying an impossible debt in the world's transactional economy – something they would have understood clearly – and contrasts it with God's economy of giving and receiving, which we call grace. This principle of debt forgiveness is etched into God's laws for Israel, with debt release every seven years, and Jubilee, every forty-nine years. Forgiveness is the cornerstone of following Christ. The financial disciple should be looking for situations in which financial debt could be forgiven.

PART 3: LEARNING FROM THE MASTER

—

CHAPTER 15

—

The Budget

Read Luke 9:12-14.

Core text

"Late in the afternoon the Twelve came to him and said, 'Send the crowd away so they can go to the surrounding villages and countryside and find food and lodging, because we are in a remote place here.' He replied, 'You give them something to eat.'

They answered, 'We have only five loaves of bread and two fish – unless we go and buy food for all this crowd.' (About five thousand men were there.)"

The disciples had been sent out by Jesus with His power and authority to preach and heal the sick. He had told them not to take anything with them, *"no staff, no bag, no bread, no money, no extra shirt"* (Luke 9:3). They travelled from village to village, presumably living off the land and hospitality from the people they met. Having been sent out in Christ's name to proclaim the Kingdom of God, I am sure they experienced God's provision during this time.

Upon their return, they told Jesus of the exciting things that had happened. Jesus, wanting some quiet time with them, took them to the small town of Bethsaida. But crowds of people found out and followed him there as well. As another day of teaching and healing grew late, the concerned disciples said, *"Send the crowds away to the nearby villages and farms, so they can find food and lodging for the night. There is nothing to eat here in this remote place"* (Luke 9:12, ESV).

The disciples had to be shocked at Jesus' response: *"You feed them!"*

I can just imagine their feelings: "Help!"

They immediately made a budget for this exercise but quickly realized they had a serious deficit. *"That would take more than half a year's wages! Are we to go and spend that much on bread and give it to them to eat?"* (Mark 6:37). Philip's mind immediately ran to the cost of the project. He quickly calculated how many man-hours of work it would take to feed all these people; he saw the task as impossible because he approached it as if everything depended on his own work and man's economy.

However, a small boy had brought his lunch – two fish and five loaves – and made it available. Jesus instructed everyone to sit down on the grass. He blessed the food and gave the fish and loaves to the disciples to distribute. The people had enough to eat and the disciples each had a basket of food left over for themselves.

Jesus' approach was completely unorthodox. Bypassing the limitations of human action plans, He used what was at hand and involved His disciples in doing the impossible. *"'Not by might nor by power, but by my Spirit,' says the Lord Almighty"* (Zechariah 4:6).

When we are asked by Jesus to do something, He will always arrange a way to pay for it. We must never reply to a command from the Lord with a weak "I can't afford it." God always pays for what He orders.

The boy started by placing what little he had into God's hands. When we invest in the Kingdom, God can multiply whatever we place into His hands – for His purposes. That is the economy of the Kingdom at work. The world economy works by percentage increase – and a very small percentage at that. But God's economy works by multiplication. If a farmer were to sow seeds and expect just a percentage increase, he would not be pleased at all; he expects the seed to multiply! Whatever God has made, He can multiply – cattle, seeds, people, products of human talent, and the earth's resources.

Because people are made in God's image, they think they should have the same power to make things multiply – including money. That's why they gamble and want to get rich quick. But only money that is invested in the Kingdom can multiply.

A widow was in serious debt and her creditors were coming to take her children as slaves. She called out to Elisha, the prophet, to help her.

"What do you have in your house?" he asked.

"Nothing," she replied, "only a little oil."

Elisha asked the widow to bring the oil to him. "Go get as many jars as you can from your neighbors and start pouring the oil into the jars."

The oil did not stop flowing until all the jars were full. "Now go and sell your oil, pay off your debts, and you and your sons can live off the rest," said Elisha.

This story in 2 Kings 4:1-7 illustrates how God can multiply whatever we place into His hands.

God will shatter the pint-sized expectations of His followers and their limitations when they bring Him what they have already been given. "Little is much when God is in it." When Christians are willing to offer their lives sacrificially, relinquishing their hold on whatever God has given them in terms of time, money, possessions and talents, God will use these ordinary things to create extraordinary events.

Jesus teaches His financial disciples to believe that their resources are never too little to serve God. God delights in taking a humble, seemingly insignificant person with little resources and using him or her for His glory.

PART 3: LEARNING FROM THE MASTER

—

CHAPTER 16

—

The Traveler

Read Luke 10:25-37.

Core text

"He went to him and bound up his wounds, pouring on oil and wine. Then he set him on his own animal and brought him to an inn and took care of him. And the next day he took out two denarii and gave them to the innkeeper, saying, 'Take care of him, and whatever more you spend, I will repay you when I come back.' Which of these three, do you think, proved to be a neighbor to the man who fell among the robbers? He said, 'The one who showed him mercy.' And Jesus said to him, 'You go, and do likewise'" (Luke 10:34-37, ESV).

When a lawyer asked what he must do to inherit eternal life, Jesus asked him what the law required. The lawyer's answer was good: *"'Love the Lord your God with all your heart and with all your soul and with all your strength and with all your mind, and your neighbor as yourself.' . . . But he wanted to justify himself, so he asked Jesus, 'And who is my neighbor?'"* (Luke 10:27-29).

Jesus cuts to the heart of the lawyer's question by telling a story lesson that is an example for everyday life.

A traveler on the road from Jerusalem to Jericho was attacked, robbed, and left half dead in the ditch. A priest passed by and ignored him. A Temple assistant looked at him and went on his way. Then a Samaritan passed by, saw him in dire straits, and showed compassion. He soothed his wound with oil and wine and dressed it. Then he put the man on his donkey and brought him to an inn where he took good care of him.

The next day he gave the innkeeper some money and asked him to care for the man. He promised to pay for any costs incurred when he returned.

This parable is a very clear answer to the lawyer's question that attempted to avoid responsibility, *"And who is my neighbor?"* After telling the story, Jesus turns the question back on the lawyer: *"Which of these three do you think was a neighbor to the man who fell into* the hands of robbers?" When the lawyer replied, *"The one who had mercy on him,"* Jesus challenged him with a clear command: *"Go and do likewise."*

The last person who would be expected to help was a Samaritan, an enemy of the Jews. But because the good man in our story was a Samaritan, Jesus is drawing a strong contrast between those who knew the law and those who actually followed the law in their lifestyle and conduct.

The lawyer's answer reveals his personal hardness of heart. He cannot bring himself to say the word "Samaritan"; he refers to the "neighbor" as *"the one who had mercy on him."* His hate for the Samaritans (his neighbors) was so strong that he couldn't even refer to them in a proper way. Jesus then tells the lawyer to *"go and do likewise,"* meaning that he should start living what the law tells him to do.

Our neighborhood is as wide as the love of God. Our neighbor is the one we meet who is in need. It's not enough to hold religious titles or positions like the priest and the Levite. It's not enough to feel a pang of remorse or sadness at someone's ill fortune. Loving your neighbor means acting on behalf of others, regardless of who they are or where they are from.

There are three main lessons in the parable of the good Samaritan.

1. We are to set aside our prejudice and priorities to show love and compassion for others.

2. Our neighbor is anyone we encounter; we are all creatures of the creator and we are to love all of mankind as Jesus has taught.

3. Keeping the law in its entirety with the intent to save ourselves is an impossible task; we need a savior, and this is Jesus.

The disciples were also learning a very practical everyday lesson: carrying out Jesus' life of mercy can cost us. The Samaritan had to stop what he was doing to help the victim. He used his assets to help the injured man.

Disregarding the possibility that the bandits may have been close by and still a threat, the Samaritan took a risk stopping to treat the injured man and transport him to the nearest inn.

He spent his money to help the traveler, who was in considerable distress. Oil and wine were not cheap. He paid for the immediate care and even gave the innkeeper a kind of blank check for whatever else might be needed. A financial disciple uses his resources to help those in need.

—

CHAPTER 17

—

The Fool

Read Luke 12:13-21.

Core text

"Then he said to them, 'Watch out! Be on your guard against all kinds of greed; life does not consist in an abundance of possessions'" (v15).

"This is how it will be with whoever stores up things for themselves but is not rich toward God" (v21).

Someone in the crowd listening to Jesus asked him to intervene in a family problem. "Tell my brother to divide our father's estate with me." In ancient times, the firstborn was guaranteed a double portion of the family inheritance. More than likely, the brother who was addressing Jesus was not the firstborn and was asking for an equal share of the inheritance rather than a third. According to Jewish custom, rabbis could settle legal disputes in the division of property between heirs. That would explain why this man came to Jesus to get a share of his brother's inheritance.

Jesus didn't want to get drawn into arbitrating their dispute, because He knew that a deeper problem existed – greed. Looking deep into the man's soul, He gets to the heart of the matter. He knows that the value this man places on his life is strongly connected with his possessions. "Watch out for all kinds of greed – your worth cannot be measured in how much you possess."

Then Jesus told the crowd a story of a rich farmer who was very successful. He was bringing in bumper crops from fertile fields. Realizing that his barns could not hold all the crops, he decided to build bigger ones. He leaned back, very satisfied with himself that he had enough to live on for many years. Time to take it easy! Eat, drink and be merry!

Presumably in a dream, God spoke to him and called him a fool, because his life was to end that night. "Then, who will get everything you worked for?" This echoes the thought expressed in Ecclesiastes 2:18-19. *"I hated all the things I had toiled for under the sun, because*

I must leave them to the one who comes after me. And who knows whether that person will be wise or foolish? Yet they will have control over all the fruit of my toil into which I have poured my effort and skill under the sun. This too is meaningless."

You see it all the time in people who are singularly devoted to the accumulation of wealth. What happens to all that wealth when they die? It gets left behind to others who didn't earn it, won't appreciate it, and will likely squander it.

Jesus told the crowds, *"A person is a fool to store up earthly wealth but not have a rich relationship with God"* (Luke 12:21, NLT).

We are not blessed by God to hoard wealth for ourselves. We are blessed to be a blessing to others and to build the kingdom of God. The Bible says, *"If riches increase, do not set your heart on them"* (Psalm 62:10, NKJV).

The consequence of being totally focused on money, is that we start to trust in what it can do for us, building up our belief in ourselves – at the cost of trusting God. Notice in the story how the rich fool talked to himself rather than to God. Notice also how many times the word "I" occurs – at least five times. Instead of serving the triune God, he was serving the unholy trinity – I, me, and myself.

It is not wrong to be rich, but prosperity should have a purpose. Writing to his disciple Timothy, Paul gives some principles to teach the rich. *"Command those who are rich in this present world not to be arrogant nor to put their hope in wealth, which is so uncertain, but to put their hope in God, who richly provides us with everything for our enjoyment. Command them to do good, to be rich in good deeds, and to be generous and willing to share. In this way they will lay up treasure for themselves as a firm foundation for the coming age, so that they may take hold of the life that is truly life"* (1 Timothy 6:17-19). That is being "rich toward God."

Greed first manifested itself with Adam and Eve in the Garden when they coveted for themselves that which was the privilege of the Creator. It still permeates our economic life today and is the root cause of most financial problems. Greed is an excessive desire to possess wealth or goods with the intention to keep them for one's self. It is an inordinate desire to acquire or possess more than one needs or deserves, especially with respect to material wealth.

Jesus teaches His financial disciples not to measure the value of their lives in terms of money or possessions but to concentrate on a rich relationship with God and to grow in service and generosity.

PART 3: LEARNING FROM THE MASTER

—

CHAPTER 18

—

The Waster

Read Luke 15:11-31.

Core text

"The younger one said to his father, 'Father, give me my share of the estate.' So he divided his property between them.

Not long after that, the younger son got together all he had, set off for a distant country and there squandered his wealth in wild living" (v 12-13).

The young man got his share of the inheritance, which would have been half of what his older brother would receive, and went off traveling. He wasted it all on wild living. When a famine broke out, he was starving and so desperate that he (a Jew!) got a job feeding pigs, but there was no food for him.

He finally came to his senses and realized that even the employees on his father's estate were living better. Full of remorse, he went back to his father to beg for forgiveness and employment as a servant, which his loving father gladly gave. The father was so pleased at his return that he organized a large feast with the son as guest of honor. The father ran to his son, greeted him with a kiss, and ordered a celebration – a picture of how our Heavenly Father feels toward sinners who repent.

The older brother was jealous and resentful of the treatment his father gave to his younger sibling. The father reassured him by saying, "You have loyally stayed with me. All I have is yours."

The younger son represents the "tax collectors and sinners" (Luke 15:1), and the elder son, the self-righteous religious people – the Pharisees and lawyers (Luke 15:2). I think we can identify with both!

This story is the third of three parables in a chapter directed at a mixed audience of tax collectors, sinners, Pharisees (religious leaders), and teachers of the law. All three parables are on the topic of lost things being found: a lost sheep, a lost coin, and a lost son. Likewise, all three parables point to the heavenly joy over every sinner who repents from sin and turns to Jesus. The main point of the story is how the father showed forgiveness, grace, and favor to the young man who repented. However, the young man is called the "Prodigal Son." Prodigal means "wastefully extravagant." Jesus also wanted to teach His financial disciples some truths about money.

The father granted the young man's request. We can learn an important lesson here. If we don't say to God, "Your will be done," then God will say to us, "Okay, then let *your* will be done!" God does not really need to punish us. Going our own way will be punishment enough! We are left to suffer the consequences of our disobedience.

The young man wasted his money, was ungrateful, and irresponsible. He showed lack of patience. He wanted the money – and wanted it now! He had no notion of waiting for what he wanted. In fact, it was usual to wait until the father died before an inheritance would be divided. Such a request is almost as if he wanted his father dead!

His bad financial management led him to a lack of even the basic necessities of life. His work yielded nothing, and he was humiliated. He recalled that the servants working loyally for his father had more than enough.

The financial problems he faced were, in fact, an outside indicator of an internal spiritual problem. The young man was very independent: he wanted to live his life as he determined. He was short-sighted, egotistical, selfish, and without discipline.

He needed to confess his wrongdoing, to turn back to his father and ask forgiveness. He needed to change course, to go back to his father's ways and enjoy his grace and provision.

It appears that the older son also needed to repent of his feeling of superiority and his anger at how his brother was received.

Perhaps a final truth Jesus wanted to teach is that it is good to enjoy all of the Lord's provision and to hold a party to celebrate something special!

Whenever we find ourselves in a tough financial spot, we can go to our Heavenly Father, confess our wrong ways, and turn back to His ways. Just like the prodigal son, we can be restored to a rich relationship with the Father.

It is much better to go to the Father and plan your finances together with Him, following His advice and accepting His provision in His time. Instead of wasting resources, the financial disciple will join in a profitable partnership with the Father.

—

CHAPTER 19

—

The Manager

Read Luke 16:1-13.

Core text

"Jesus told his disciples: 'There was a rich man whose manager was accused of wasting his possessions. So he called him in and asked him, "What is this I hear about you? Give an account of your management, because you cannot be manager any longer"'" (v 1-2). "I tell you, use worldly wealth to gain friends for yourselves, so that when it is gone, you will be welcomed into eternal dwellings. Whoever can be trusted with very little can also be trusted with much, and whoever is dishonest with very little will also be dishonest with much" (v 9-10).

The manager was accused of mishandling the rich man's affairs. About to be fired, he was asked to give a report of his accounting. With only a small window of time and opportunity to secure his uncertain future, the manager wanted to gain and leverage friends that he hoped would repay his favorable treatment.

He turned customers into friends by forgiving up to 50 percent of their debt to his master. Even the rich master commended the manager for being shrewd.

Jesus used the story to get the attention of his listeners and to make a point. The point is that all of us have a small amount of time (compared to eternity) and a small amount of resources (compared to God). As followers of Jesus, we should leverage our time and resources on earth to maximize God's Kingdom.

When worldly people use their small amounts of time and money to create a secure future for themselves here on earth, Jesus said that they are "more shrewd" than the "children of the light" or followers of God. Why? Because as followers of Jesus, we should know that we are foreigners here for a short amount of time and that our best use of worldly wealth is to benefit others and introduce them to eternity (v 9). Entrance into eternity comes only through forgiveness and grace. When people hear the good news of the gospel, they have an opportunity to go through a heavenly door they never knew existed. We can use our money to help facilitate this.

Jesus then goes on to share how he evaluates our honesty and trustworthiness: He looks at the way we handle money! Imagine Him looking into your eyes and asking questions like these:

- Are you faithful with the little you have?

- Are you trustworthy in handling worldly wealth?

- Are you to be trusted with someone else's property?

If you are found to be trustworthy and faithful, then Jesus says He can trust you with much, with "true riches" and with "property of your own."

After that, Jesus gives a choice: you can love God and be devoted to Him in all your financial dealings, or you can hate and despise Him by choosing to love and be devoted to money. The Pharisees had already made their choice. In verse 14 we read, "The Pharisees, who loved money, heard all this and were sneering at Jesus."

Jesus is asking us as His disciples to use money to introduce people to the Kingdom of God. This parable is all about getting prepared for the future, a future in which we are about to be removed from this world to meet our Maker and account for our management of the resources He entrusted to us. Our time on earth is short, but the new reality that follows it will last forever. With such an obvious contrast, Jesus wants us to get serious about preparing for eternity!

A financial disciple understands that the ultimate goal is to use money for God's purposes, leveraging every opportunity while on earth to help people enter His Kingdom. Since taking possessions to heaven is not an option, the best way to use them is to benefit others who may become heavenly friends who will welcome us to our eternal home. This is the ultimate win-win.

PART 3: LEARNING FROM THE MASTER

—

CHAPTER 20

—

The
Rich Man

Read Luke 16:19-31.

Core text

"There was a rich man who was dressed in purple and fine linen and lived in luxury every day. At his gate was laid a beggar named Lazarus, covered with sores and longing to eat what fell from the rich man's table. Even the dogs came and licked his sores. The time came when the beggar died and the angels carried him to Abraham's side. The rich man also died and was buried" (v 19-22).

After teaching His disciples about the steward, Jesus said, *"No servant can serve two masters, for either he will hate the one and love the other, or he will be devoted to the one and despise the other. You cannot serve God and money"* (Luke 16:13).

Some Pharisees – Jewish religious leaders – heard Him say this. They loved money and sneered at Jesus, who told them, *"You are the ones who justify yourselves in the eyes of others, but God knows your hearts. What people value highly is detestable in God's sight"* (Luke 16:15).

Jesus then told a story in the Pharisees' hearing about a rich man dressed in expensive purple cloth and fine linen who held lavish parties. Near the rich man's gate was a poor, sick beggar named Lazarus, who wished only for some crumbs to eat. They both died.

Each of us will die sometime – maybe soon, maybe many years from now. What we read about the rich man and Lazarus should encourage us and serve as a warning.

The Bible says there is a heaven (Paradise) and a separate and eternal hell, a terrible place of torment. We read that Lazarus found himself in heaven next to Abraham, the ancient Hebrew patriarch who founded the Israelites, God's chosen people.

Imagine what heaven was like for Lazarus! Quite a change from lying on a stretcher with sores covering his body and dogs licking at his sores. He was in heaven for eternity, where there is no death and no pain.

The rich man, however, went to hell, where he suffered and pleaded for mercy. But It was too late. While on earth, the rich man pursued earthly wealth and its benefits. In serving wealth, he used people. This continued even after he died, as he implored Abraham to send Lazarus to warn his brothers. But his concern for his brothers doesn't seem to extend to people like Lazarus or wishing to submit to God and rectify his lifetime of callous disregard.

Life after death is a hotly debated topic. What happens after we die? How do our lives on earth affect how we spend eternity? This story, coupled with the good news of the gospel, tells us that what we believe and place our faith in during our earthly lives determines our eternal destiny. If we place our faith in anything other than God — including money and possessions — we will be left with nothing and spend eternity in hell separated from God. But if we place our faith in Jesus Christ, we will spend eternity in His presence.

The other key theme of this passage deals with riches and poverty. Poor people have coexisted with rich people since humankind's earliest days. It is not wrong to be rich or poor. However, in the Bible, God says that earthly wealth is temporary and is provided for us to meet our needs and also the needs of others. He wants His followers to lovingly, compassionately, and generously use their resources to help people in need.

Jesus condemned the rich man for his *use* of wealth, not for *having* wealth. Instead of helping hurting people like Lazarus (who received bad things in life), the rich man (who received good things in life), squandered them all in pursuing his selfish desires.

Contrary to what our culture wants us to believe, the financial goal of Christians should never be focused on having easy, comfortable lives. In a way, as followers of Christ, we are called to be like God's hands and feet among needy people, wisely sharing our resources. We do this in our neighborhoods, in nursing homes and retirement centers, in homeless shelters, with families struggling to survive financially, and with people who cannot afford proper medical care.

Jesus wants his financial disciples to use their money to show grace to needy people.

—

CHAPTER 21

—

The Leader

Read Luke 18:18-30.

Core text

"And he [the leader] said, 'All these [commandments] I have kept from my youth.' When Jesus heard this, he said to him, 'One thing you still lack. Sell all that you have and distribute to the poor, and you will have treasure in heaven; and come, follow me'" (v 21-22, ESV).

A leader came to Jesus with a sincere question: *"Good Teacher, what must I do to inherit eternal life?"* The young man did not recognize with whom he was talking. The young ruler saw Jesus as a moral man, a man of insight and depth, but did not recognise His divine authority. To make such a mistake is fatal.

The young leader replied that he had kept all of the commandments since he was a boy. Seeing right through him to his soul, Jesus laid His finger on the sore spot. The man's problem lay in the fact that he had not kept the first commandment: *"You shall have no other gods before me."* But the young leader served another god, the power of money. Jesus gave him a radical solution to this deeper problem of idolatry. *"You still lack one thing. Sell everything you have and give to the poor, and you will have treasure in heaven. Then come, follow me"* (v 22). But the rich, young ruler, like most other Pharisees (See Luke 16:14), was a lover of money. He broke the very first commandment, *"You shall have no other gods before me"* (Exodus 20:3).

The young man addressed Jesus as "Good Teacher." He will not be able to understand anything else Jesus will tell him unless he grasps that our relative standards of goodness are much, much different from God's absolute goodness and His standards of righteousness. In coming to Jesus and talking about money and possessions, we don't merely need a Good Teacher, we need a Savior. We don't merely need information on how to manage our money, we need deliverance from the power of money in our lives. The root of the young man's problem was love of money.

The Lord made a frontal attack on the young man's weakness – the sins of covetousness, indulgence, and materialism. Overcome with sadness at the thought of losing his great wealth, the young ruler ran into a brick wall. Jewish teachers reckon this man was a highly influential member of the Sanhedrin, the highest Jewish council. In Jewish theology at the time, wealth was considered synonymous with God's blessing. Giving that up would be seen by others as a sign that God was not pleased with him. Giving up wealth also meant relinquishing his place in Jewish society, his status and influence.

As a Pharisee, a teacher of the law, the young leader should have known the Scriptures, particularly Proverbs 19:17, *"Whoever is kind to the poor lends to the Lord, and he will reward them for what they have done."* He should have realized that giving all to the poor would be making a loan to God, a loan to be repaid with a reward. It seems like the belly of the poor is a much safer investment than the bank!

The young man thinks he has kept all the commandments but still senses a lack, an incompleteness, or else he wouldn't have come to Jesus in the first place. Although Jesus speaks very specifically to the young man's point of need, the young man seems to think that the cure is worse than his disease. Jesus proposes selling all his property and giving the proceeds to those who are least able to reciprocate, the poor. James is right when he characterizes true religion: *"Religion that God our Father accepts as pure and faultless is this: to look after orphans and widows in their distress and to keep oneself from being polluted by the world"* (James 1:27).

Jesus' answer to the man is very unsettling to many of us. Why are we so worried about it? Do we, too, feel possessive of what we have? Do we fear that Jesus may require us to do something that would cost us too much? What do we fear? And why? We fear because we sense that we have not fully surrendered. Jesus' words to the rich young ruler are quite consistent with what he has been saying to his disciples throughout his journeys: *"Those of you who do not give up everything you have cannot be my disciples"* (Luke 14:33).

This is a first requirement for the financial disciple – renouncing all we have and surrendering to the Lord's will. Jesus did just that. He surrendered presence, power, position, prestige . . . He gave up all to come live among us, to serve us, and even die for us. We need to cut the umbilical cord that ties us to money and possessions, placing everything at the foot of the cross for the Lord to do with as He pleases.

PART 3: LEARNING FROM THE MASTER

—

CHAPTER 22

—

The Tax Man

Read Luke 19:1-9.

Core text

"Zacchaeus stood up and said to the Lord, 'Look, Lord! Here and now I give half of my possessions to the poor, and if I have cheated anybody out of anything, I will pay back four times the amount.' Jesus said to him, 'Today salvation has come to this house'" (v 8-9).

Zacchaeus was not merely a tax collector. He was in charge of collecting Roman taxes for a whole region and had many people working for him. A chief tax collector would be appointed to collect a given sum from a district. He would be permitted to add a charge for raising the amount specified by the Romans. The chief tax collector would divide his district into areas and appoint area tax collectors. They would have to collect enough money to satisfy both the Romans and the chief tax collector.

Excessive Roman taxes were a huge burden. Tax collectors were protected by the Roman occupiers for whom they worked, but no laws protected the hard-working taxpayers.

Zacchaeus became rich by using his position to take excessive tax overrides. This unfairly impoverished many, making them resentful of this man who was stealing from them. Since he had the full support of the Roman authorities, people were powerless to stop him.

Zacchaeus was far from living up to the name his parents had given him, which means "pure and innocent." Instead, he was greedy and guilty. Considered a traitor to his nation and loathed by the people despite being one of them, a "son of Abraham," he was stealing from his own people.

Many tax collectors had come earlier to John the Baptist to be baptized, and asked, *"'Teacher, what shall we do?' And he said to them, 'Collect no more than you are authorized to do'"* (Luke 3:12-13, ESV). They were to be honest in all their dealings. Clearly, Zacchaeus had ignored this. The basic requirement of paying taxes and giving to Caesar what belongs to Caesar was later confirmed by Jesus. However, Zacchaeus was extorting large sums from people and was filthy rich.

Zacchaeus, probably disgusted with himself and needing a savior, wanted to see Jesus. He was certainly innovative, climbing a tree to get a good view. Sensing his desire, Jesus called him by name. *"Zacchaeus, come down immediately. I must stay at your house today"* (v 5). Zacchaeus was excited and joyful at Jesus' words, although the people watching were very displeased that Jesus would be the guest of a notorious sinner.

When Jesus comes into a home, everything changes! Hearts change and home economics change.

Zacchaeus knew the biblical laws of restitution, and he placed his money where his mouth was. *"When they sin in any of these ways and realize their guilt, they must return what they have stolen or taken by extortion, or what was entrusted to them . . . They must make restitution in full, add a fifth of the value to it and give it all to the owner"* (Leviticus 6:4-5).

Genuine repentance leads to a desire to make wrongs right. A financial disciple will develop a desire born of deep conviction to do good, and that includes making restitution whenever possible. Restitution is to be a *result* of our salvation — it is not a *requirement* for salvation. Spiritual conversion must be accompanied by practical economic repentance and conversion. Zacchaeus acknowledged his guilt, was remorseful, and committed to make restitution. From Jesus' words, we know that he was forgiven and restored as a true son of Abraham.

For the financial disciple, especially ones in a leadership position like Zacchaeus, absolute honesty is a core element of every single decision regarding money, how to deal with people, and how to manage money God's way.

One Bible verse I memorized a long time ago has been a guiding principle throughout my business career of forty years: *"You shall*

not steal; you shall not deal falsely; you shall not lie to one another"
(Leviticus 19:11, ESV). This basic requirement for a financial disciple is
clear and non-negotiable.

PART 3: LEARNING FROM THE MASTER

—

CHAPTER 23

—

The Market

Read Mark 11:15-18.

Core text

"Jesus entered the temple courts and began driving out those who were buying and selling there. He overturned the tables of the money changers and the benches of those selling doves, and would not allow anyone to carry merchandise through the temple courts" (v 15-16).

Jesus entered Jerusalem to spend the last week leading up to His capture and death on the cross. One of the first things He did when entering the Temple was to drive out all who were changing money and buying and selling animals for sacrifices. He would not allow anyone with merchandise through the temple courts.

This was an aggressive act with which we would not normally associate Jesus. He was visibly angry.

You could argue that the businesspeople were conducting a reasonable profession. Pilgrims arriving in Jerusalem from many different nations needed to exchange their money. Believers wanted to buy animals to sacrifice in the temple. So, what was the problem?

Judea was under the rule of the Romans, and Roman coin was the currency. Jewish law required that every man should pay a tribute to the service of the sanctuary of "half a shekel," a Jewish coin. It became, therefore, a matter of convenience to have a place where the Roman coin could be exchanged for the Jewish half-shekel. Moneychangers provided this convenience but would demand a commission for the exchange. Because so many thousands of people came up to the great feasts, changing money was a very profitable business. It is said that the rate of exchange was inflated, resulting in oppression for the pilgrims.

Two doves or pigeons were required to be offered in sacrifice, yet it was not always possible to bring them from distant parts, so another lucrative business sprang up: sellers charged exorbitant prices for the birds, cattle, and sheep for temple sacrifices – many of which were second-rate.

Jesus was filled with righteous indignation. As He overturned the tables of the moneychangers, He condemned them for having turned God's house of prayer into *"a den of thieves."*

Three years earlier, Jesus did the very same thing, as we can read in John 2:13-17. He seemed at that time to be even more angry, as He used a whip, overturned tables, and scattered the coins on the ground.

The place in the temple where this occurred is significant. The cleansing took place in the "court of the Gentiles." In addition to the areas reserved to the members of the people of Israel, there was a space in which everyone could enter, Jews and non-Jews, circumcised and uncircumcised, members or not of the chosen people, people educated in the law and people who weren't. Here, the rabbis and teachers of the law gathered, ready to listen to people's questions about God and to respond in a respectful and compassionate exchange. It was the area in the temple where anyone was permitted to come to learn about God and receive grace.

That's why Jesus was consumed by zeal for God's house. The economy of the world works by buying and selling, which is subject to dishonesty, wrongdoing, manipulation and greed, as we saw in the temple court. The economy of the Kingdom of God works by giving and receiving, which we call grace. The business people were consumed by money; Jesus was consumed by love for the Father.

It is no wonder that Mark's account goes on to say, *"When the leading priests and teachers of religious law heard what Jesus had done, they began planning how to kill him"* (Mark 11:18, NLT).

Financial disciples need to constantly evaluate all their economic dealings to be sure they are serving the Lord and not money. When gaining, using, and investing money becomes the number one focus, they are serving money.

The goal of our work and business must not be to make money! We work to love and glorify God and to serve others with the gifts and talents He has given us. God provides – not the marketplace, not our employer.

In our money management, whether earning, spending, or accumulating, all our transactions must be done prayerfully, honestly, and for God-given goals.

—

CHAPTER 24

—

The Investors

Read Luke 19:11-27.

Core text

"So he called ten of his servants and gave them ten minas. 'Put this money to work,' he said, 'until I come back'" (v 13).

Jesus wanted to tell people a story about the Kingdom of God because they thought that the Kingdom would appear immediately, and that an earthly kingdom of Israel would soon be established. However, He was on His way to Jerusalem to die. A very different Kingdom would be founded. To illustrate this, Jesus told of a man of high birth who went into a faraway country to receive for himself a kingdom and then return. He called ten of his servants and gave them ten minas with an assignment to put the money to work until he returns.

Two of the servants take the risk of investing their master's money. They earn handsome returns. A third servant is afraid to take the risk, so he puts the money in a safe place. It earns no return. When the master returns, he has become king of the whole territory. He rewards the two servants who made money for him, promoting them to high positions of their own. He punishes the servant who kept the money safe but unproductive.

In this parable, Jesus is showing how He will compensate servants who have the same opportunities but manifest different degrees of faithfulness. A mina was a Greek monetary unit worth one hundred denarii or about four months' wages for an average worker based on a six-day work week. The minas in the parable are representative of resources God gives us to do the work of His Kingdom on earth.

This parable could well have been told with actual events in mind. A Jewish nobleman (Archelaus, son of Herod) had actually gone into a far country (Rome) to receive a kingdom (Judea). He had been hated by his subjects for his terrible cruelty, and he had massacred thousands. They sent a delegation after him, saying, "We will not have this man reign over us." He was, however, given lordship over Judea, and returned to reward his followers who had enriched themselves and him at the expense of the people, and to punish cruelly all who opposed him. It is as though Jesus was saying to the crowds, "Do you really want a king? Remember what happened with Archelaus?"

Jesus was to go away and then return to establish His Kingdom, which was the very opposite of that of Archelaus! It was to be a good Kingdom in which Christ reigns in the hearts of His followers. The subjects who rejected the nobleman in the parable were clearly the people of Israel.

The two servants who invested their money well are the faithful financial disciples. Faithful because they obeyed the command to *"put this money to work."* The servant who hid the money is an unfaithful disciple.

It appears as though disciples who manage well what has been entrusted to them will receive incredible rewards. All of the servants were given the same resources, but not all were able to use them to the same degree. We do not all have the same capabilities, gifts, or talents, but we will be held accountable for what we do with the resources God has given to us. The third servant should at the very least have put the money in the bank to earn interest. Instead, he reacted in fear, wrapped the money in cloth, and did nothing productive with it.

"I was afraid of you, because you are a hard man. You take out what you did not put in and reap what you did not sow" (v 21). This makes more sense if we see Archelaus — not Jesus — as the nobleman-become-king in the parable. The parable king is a corrupt ruler and representative of the world system. We are to be faithful in using our resources well in the midst of a corrupt society.

Notice that the reward of good stewardship is even greater stewardship responsibilities. When our Master sees a financial disciple who is faithful and diligent, He entrusts that person with more responsibility.

God is an investor with expectations. He invests in us and expects a return of fruitfulness on His investment. The fruit of our labors is then returned to God as the Owner and Provider.

—

CHAPTER 25

—

The Government

Read Luke 20:19-26.

Core text

"'Show Me a denarius. Whose image and inscription does it have?'

They answered and said, 'Caesar's.' And He said to them, 'Render therefore to Caesar the things that are Caesar's, and to God the things that are God's'" (v 24-25, NKJV).

Jesus gave this brilliant answer to some religious leaders who tried to trap him with a question for which any answer he might give could create serious trouble for him from one authority or another.

They asked, *"Is it lawful for us to pay taxes to Caesar or not?"* (v 22, NKJV). In other words, "Should we pay taxes to this Gentile government, or should we withhold them?"

Jesus, knowing their hypocrisy, said to them, "Why put me to the test? Bring me a denarius and let me look at it." And they brought one. And he said to them, "Whose likeness and inscription is this?" They said to him, "Caesar's." Jesus said to them, *"Render therefore to Caesar the things that are Caesar's, and to God the things that are God's."* And they marvelled at him.

What is God's? Everything. So the point seems to be that when you realize that all of life, including all of Caesar's rights and power and possessions, belong to God, then you will be in a proper frame of mind to render to Caesar what is due to Caesar. When you know that all is God's, then anything you render to Caesar will be done for God's sake. Any authority you ascribe to Caesar you will ascribe to him for the sake of God's greater authority. Any obedience you render to Caesar you will render for the sake of the obedience you owe first to God. Any claim Caesar makes on you, you test by the infinitely higher claim God has on you.

What belongs to Caesar is determined by the fact that everything is God's first; it only becomes Caesar's by God's permission and design.

Only God decides what is a rightful, limited rendering to Caesar. The only reason God ordains the rights of a Caesar is to accomplish His own plan.

Therefore, Peter could say, *"Be subject for the Lord's sake to every human institution, whether it be to the emperor as supreme, or to governors as sent by him . . ."* (1 Peter 2:13-14, ESV).

Jesus and Peter are calling for Christians to have the mindset of an alien and a citizen at the same time. *"Live as people who are free, not using your freedom as a cover-up for evil, but living as servants of God"* (1 Peter 2:16, ESV). We are God's servants, not the servants of any government. We are free from all governments and human institutions because we belong to the Owner of the universe and share in that inheritance (*"fellow heirs with Christ"*). God has made us and bought us for Himself.

Being freed from the world and from Caesar, God sends us for a season back into the foreign structures and institutions of society to be *"faithful in that which is another's"* (Luke 16:12, ESV). We are to live out the alien ideas of another Kingdom in the midst of our earthly homeland. There will always be tension as we live in these two kingdoms.

This is stewardship in action. I like to pay the tax that belongs to the government – first of all because I love God and want to respect His will. And because paying taxes is an act of obedience, it means I have to be completely honest in my tax returns. I have to admit that I have not been very faithful to this in the past. There is a great temptation to conceal some income. However, honesty and truth are prerequisites for God's blessing.

The second reason I am thankful to pay taxes is that it means I am earning something. This is a sign of God's provision.

As a financial disciple, you will thank God for the income He has provided, even though you may think it isn't enough. Remember, God makes no mistakes. Thank God for the way in which you can help facilitate the work of the government to provide necessary services through your taxes. God provides so that you can also meet the needs of others; this includes all your fellow citizens. Turn your tax return into an offer of thanks to God!

All that this world provides has been entrusted to us by God in stewardship. All that the next world offers has been purchased for us by Another, by Jesus himself, through His sacrificial death. It becomes our own through the obedience of faith. As we demonstrate trustworthiness with the material things of this world, God entrusts to us the true treasures – not because we deserve them but because God has graced them to us in and through Jesus. To base our lives on this truth is to demonstrate real wisdom.

—

CHAPTER 26

—

The Widow

Read Mark 12:41-44.

Core text

"They all gave out of their wealth; but she, out of her poverty, put in everything – all she had to live on" (v 44).

The scene is the temple in Jerusalem. Jesus had given His disciples a stern warning about the teachers of the law. *"They like to walk around in flowing robes and be greeted with respect in the marketplaces, and have the most important seats in the synagogues and the places of honor at banquets. They devour widows' houses and for a show make lengthy prayers. These men will be punished most severely"* (Mark 12:38-40).

They loved to be seen and heard and publicly honored. However, they used widows for their own personal gain. Then Jesus comes with an example of what He considers most important. The religious officials of the day, instead of helping the widows in need, were perfectly content to rob them of their livelihood and inheritance. The system was corrupt, and the darkness of the scribes' greed makes the widow's sacrifice shine even more brightly.

Jesus sat down in the temple and watched people bring their offerings to the treasury. This took place in the court of women, which held thirteen receptacles for people to cast their money into as they walked by. The trumpet-shaped receptacles magnified the sound of falling coins, much to the pride of those giving many to impress anyone watching.

The woman brought two small copper coins, a mere tinkle drowned out by the clatter in neighboring receptacles.

But God sees what man overlooks. The rich people threw their gifts into the receptacle, making sure that every motion was seen and every jingle heard as the coins tumbled down. Cha-ching! People paid no attention to what the widow was giving – but Jesus did.

God evaluates donations differently, not on the basis of what we give, but what we keep. The rich gave out of their abundance; the widow gave out of her poverty. The rich had not begun to give at the level of sacrifice; the widow offered a true sacrifice.

God commends giving in faith. This dear woman is supporting the temple and its corrupt system with her perseverance in true faith, despite having been ravaged by that very system. She gave *"all she had to live on."*

Instead of asking for charity from the temple, the widow was contributing the last of her money, fully believing that the Lord would take care of her. Like the widow of Zarephath in 1 Kings 17:8–16 who gave her last meal to Elijah, the widow in the temple gave away her last means of self-support. Does this mean the widow left the temple completely destitute, went home, and died of starvation? I don't think so! I think she enjoyed God's provision of her daily needs as Jesus promised in Matthew 6:25-34.

It is interesting to read that Jesus sat down to watch. He was looking, not at the amount the people were giving, but at their heart's attitude. Were they giving to uphold a reputation or because they loved God?

We should consider that Jesus is watching how we give today. Are we giving out of duty, tradition, or personal reasons like the rich in the temple? Or are we giving sacrificially because we love God and depend on Him for all we need?

The financial disciple realizes that God gives to us so that we can give. *"Each one must give as he has decided in his heart, not reluctantly or under compulsion, for God loves a cheerful giver. And God is able to make all grace abound to you, so that having all sufficiency in all things at all times, you may abound in every good work"* (2 Corinthians 9:7-8, ESV).

Therefore, the financial disciple can also give sacrificially. Jesus doesn't tell the woman to keep her money; He lets her give and His heart is almost swelling with thankfulness for this lady. If He stops her, he deprives her of the blessing of giving to God. So He lets her do it. Know that when you make sacrifices for God, He is watching. It doesn't matter if no one else sees or knows. In fact, it is better if they don't. But you may count on the fact that God sees and knows your giving. Jesus promises, *". . . Your Father, who sees what is done in secret, will reward you"* (Matthew 6:4).

Many people ask me about the tithe, giving ten percent of income to God's work. My first reaction is, "Let's talk first about giving one-hundred percent to God! Get that right, and the ten percent will take care of itself!" The widow knew that: she gave the one hundred percent. *"Each one must give as he has decided in his heart, not reluctantly or under compulsion, for God loves a cheerful giver."*

—

CHAPTER 27

—

The Traitor

Read Luke 22:3-6.

Core text

"And Judas went to the chief priests and the officers of the temple guard and discussed with them how he might betray Jesus. They were delighted and agreed to give him money" (v 5).

It seems as though Jesus knew that Judas would betray him right from the very beginning. The disciple John in his Gospel states, *". . . Jesus knew from the beginning who those were who did not believe, and who it was who would betray him"* (John 6:64, ESV).

Then Peter spoke up and said, *"We have believed, and have come to know, that you are the Holy One of God."* Jesus responds, *"Did I not choose you, the twelve? And yet one of you is a devil."* Jesus was referring to Judas.

Later, when Mary anoints Jesus' feet with expensive ointment, Judas complained that the ointment could have been sold for 300 days' wages, with the money given to the poor. But John explains that Judas's complaint was not motivated by concern for the poor. Rather, it was his own self-interest, because he *"was a thief, and having charge of the moneybag he used to help himself to what was put into it"* (John 12:4-6, ESV).

Judas was in financial bondage from the very start.

The world economy runs by buying and selling; in contrast, the Kingdom economy runs by giving and receiving. The world economy is a transactional economy determined by the laws of buying and selling. The economy of the Kingdom is covenantal, relational, determined by grace. Entrance cannot be bought; it is freely given to those who want to receive Christ's offer.

Jesus allowed himself to become subject to the laws and power of the world's economy at the cross. He was sold by Judas for hard cash and bought by the Pharisees for thirty silver pieces. At the cross of Christ, all the powers were present to celebrate his death. There was political power in the form of Pontius Pilate, the Roman governor; military power in the form of Roman soldiers; religious power represented by the Pharisees; and financial power, represented by Judas. Thank God, those powers could not prevail. Jesus allowed Himself to be subject to them once and for all so that by His death and resurrection all these powers could be defeated, and we could enter into His victory!

While attending a conference, one of the main speakers made a passing comment in his presentation that sent shivers down my spine. The speaker said, "Judas betrayed Jesus for money." For the first time in my entire life I found myself painfully identifying with Judas, the betrayer.

I had often related to Peter, who was too bold and carelessly impetuous. And to Samson, with his great strength but lack of self-control. And even to King Saul, who *played the fool.* But never before had I seen myself in Judas, the betrayer — until that moment.

The word "betray" means to "turn someone over to another," the way a police officer would turn over a convict to a prison warden. I asked myself, "Has my life or my behavior ever turned Jesus over to be mocked, ridiculed, or punished by another because of my hypocritical, uncontrolled, self-centered life?"

In business I have, to my shame, done things that did not bring honor to God. I have allowed what seemed like a more urgent need for money to override my conscience and make me a traitor to Him. I hate to think what the people who experienced my shameful actions would think about the Jesus I serve.

When Jesus chose His disciples, Luke said that Judas would become a "traitor," meaning "someone who is false to a duty or an obligation." None of us would like to think of ourselves as traitors to Christ. But think about it. Have you ever been inconsistent in a duty or an obligation to Christ because His will didn't align with yours? Have you ever abandoned His business for your own because your business looked more profitable? Have you ever been guilty of dereliction of duty to Him in your financial dealings with others? These sobering questions may help you recall times in which you have indeed been a traitor to Him.

Instead of being a traitor, you as a financial disciple should be the opposite. Loyal at all times and in all circumstances, obedient to all the Master is asking you to do regardless of the cost. In His sermon on money and our daily needs (Matthew 6:24-33), Jesus gives three clear guidelines: choose God over money, trust Him to provide, and don't worry. Do your part and God will do His.

—

CHAPTER 28

—

A Map and a Compass

The life journey of a financial disciple is an unknown. It may be confusing, difficult, and at times extremely challenging. In front of us may be potholes and debris that could result in injury. The path may resemble an unmarked highway with detours. It is all so confusing. Which way shall I go? What road shall I take? To navigate our journey, we need a map and a compass.

A compass is an instrument used for orientation and navigation that shows direction relative to north. No matter where you are on a journey, you can look at your compass and it will always point to the north, a fixed point that never changes. When it is dark, cloudy, or when you are surrounded by water, the compass always enables you to determine what direction you're facing. It is simple to use and very reliable.

To navigate successfully, you also need a map. A map shows you where you want to go, and a compass helps you get there. Your map is, of course, the Word of God, the Bible, which points you to Christlikeness. The Bible is an accurate map that shows you the landscape in which you travel as a disciple. The compass guides you relative to true north, God Himself. Our compass is the Compass biblical teaching on stewardship that will help you navigate your finances – God's way!

The needle on a compass always points north. If you know where you want to go, you can lay a compass on a map and it will give you the right direction to take, for example, "go northwest" or "travel in a southwesterly direction."

When navigating the journey of a financial disciple, biblical teaching gives you the route to travel. Here is a model I have used to teach people on the journey of financial discipleship. It consists of eight compass points, each leading to the development of a competency essential to navigating your finances – God's way.

Every compass point is relative to true north – the biblical truth about God: His ownership of everything and the fact that we have been appointed His stewards.

You may want to spend more time going in one direction than another, but all directions are important and should be traveled. At certain times on your journey, one compass point will be more needed than others.

The diagram's waypoints are set up to be traveled clockwise. When you have traveled all the waypoints and return back to north, you start again, evaluating your progress while still referring to true north. You will only end your journey when you meet Jesus face to face. Then He will evaluate what you have done with the resources He has entrusted to you. Until then, you continue refining your financial discipleship by revisiting all the compass points along your journey.

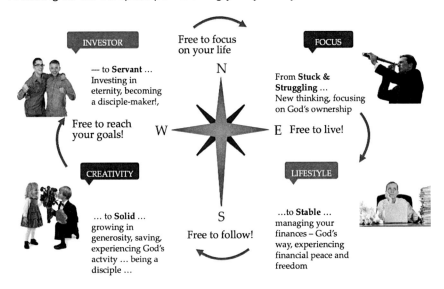

The first Compass points, from north to east, help focus on God's values, His ownership, and overcoming the spiritual power of money.

The Compass points from East to South offer practical teaching about navigating your finances – God's way.

With that foundation in place, the Compass points from South to West help you experience contentment and satisfaction, growing in generosity, and reaching your long-term goals.

Then, traveling Compass points from West to North will help you invest in eternity by assisting others to move from success to significance as financial disciples.

Once you complete the cycle for yourself, your focus enlarges to helping others utilize the map and the compass.

Ideally, the map becomes a continuous, multi-dimensional loop that (1) improves yourself, (2) improves others, and (3) further multiplies financial disciples.

CHAPTER 29

—

Compass Point North: The Gold Standard

In 1717 as "Master of the Mint" of the British government, Isaac Newton fixed the price of one ounce of gold at £3 17s 10 ½ d. This Gold Standard dominated economics for well over 200 years. The value of paper money was fixed to this standard. Everyone knew what a British pound was worth. Britain abandoned the standard after the depression in 1931, and its counterpart in America was interred in 1971 by President Nixon. Our day-to-day use of money is now decoupled from anything that has intrinsic value. Money is now only a promise from a government and worth only the ability of that government to honor its promises.

The past fifty years have brought us prosperity but also greed, speculation, and manipulation through leveraging other people's money. Our faith in banks and politicians has eroded. This has led to devaluing money by printing more and more currency and to spiralling debt through buying with "free" money. Confidence in government's promises is low.

Financial disciples should get back on the spiritual "Gold Standard," which is based on the solid promises of God!

There is something of intrinsic and eternal worth that measures everything we think, feel, and do regarding money. It is a rich, timeless, biblical perspective on money that measures and tests our spending and saving, giving and borrowing, financial planning, and lifestyle. It is our God Standard!

Getting back on the God Standard focuses on asking God to reveal His plans for my financial life. A prerequisite is realizing that God owns everything and that He has an opinion on how we should be using His assets. The first directional point that our compass will lead us to is true north – a point that never changes, making navigation possible. True north is the never-changing, infallible Word of God. If my relationship with God is the most important thing in my life, then I want to focus my energy, my time, and my resources on Him. Focusing on God's values becomes vital in managing my money and possessions; His standards become mine.

Problems and challenge

Many churches are experiencing financial problems. Projects get put on the back burner because church leaders are anxious about income. Giving is withheld or reduced and talk of generosity seems inappropriate. We focus on ourselves and we make decisions, especially financial ones, in a privatized way, excluding God from them.

This is a telling picture of an affluent society. We work harder for longer hours and have more than ever before – yet we are not satisfied.

The prophet Haggai challenges the people to consider their lifestyles and the choices they make about their standard of living. *"'Thus says the Lord of hosts: These people say the time has not yet come to rebuild the house of the Lord.' Then the word of the Lord came by the hand of Haggai the prophet, 'Is it a time for you yourselves to dwell in your paneled houses, while this house lies in ruins?'"* (Haggai 1:3-4, ESV). I think the "paneled houses" are a reference to the richly polished wooden panels that often decorate the homes of the wealthy. Not everyone has them, but we would all like them.

Haggai's issue is really everyone's issue – in the home, church, business community, etc., where "my house" and "my money" are higher priorities than "God's house."

Haggai goes on to sketch the people's problem. *"Now, therefore, thus says the Lord of hosts: Consider your ways. You have sown much and harvested little. You eat, but you never have enough; you drink, but you never have your fill. You clothe yourselves, but no one is warm. And he who earns wages does so to put them into a bag with holes"* (Haggai 1:5-6, ESV).

God often uses His withholding of provision to get our attention. When all our hard work seems to be for nothing, it may be God's invitation to consider our ways: are we adjusting our lives to His ways? After being back in Jerusalem for sixteen years following exile to Babylon, God complained that the people were still not seeking His ways. If we go through tough times, let's be thankful that God doesn't leave us alone; He intervenes.

Haggai's picture of bags with holes is a powerful image. In a recession, we generally begin to spend less as we get more conservative and rein in our use of credit. But I think the message of Haggai runs deeper. God does not want us to just patch up our bags and wait for things to get back to normal. Instead, we must find a new way of living as faithful stewards of all that God has given to us. Don't patch the inferior bags; get new bags!

God challenged the people through Haggai. *"Thus says the Lord of hosts: Consider your ways. Go up to the hills and bring wood and build the house, that I may take pleasure in it and that I may be glorified, says the Lord. You looked for much, and behold, it came to little. And when you brought it home, I blew it away. Why? declares the Lord of hosts. Because of my house that lies in ruins, while each of you busies himself with his own house"* (Haggai 1:7-9, ESV).

He challenges us today to consider our ways, to deny self and to build His house!

Getting back on the Go(l)d standard

The basis for getting back onto the God standard is acknowledging God's ownership. Haggai states clearly, *". . . I will fill this house with glory, says the Lord of hosts. The silver is mine, and the gold is mine, declares the Lord of hosts"* (Haggai 2:7-8, ESV).

The Bible is clear that *everything* belongs to God. *"The earth is the Lord's, and everything in it, the world, and all who live in it"* (Psalm 24:1). *"Who has a claim against me that I must pay? Everything under heaven belongs to me"* (Job 41:11).

You also belong to God, having been redeemed, bought back from the world. *". . . You are not your own, for you were bought with a price . . ."* (1 Corinthians 6:19-20, ESV).

An ad for the very expensive Philippe Patek watch stated, "You never actually own it, you merely take care of it for the next generation."

Actually, you never really own anything! When we think of the benefits of ownership, we usually think of having complete access to something, taking care of it and using it for good. Consider this; if you didn't own *anything*, but had access to virtually *everything* this planet and humanity can offer, you would have more than the richest people on this planet will *ever* have. The whole planet would be yours to use. Relinquishing ownership to God opens a door for you to access the Kingdom and all it can offer.

Some people try to own as much as possible, thinking this will bring the best lifestyle for them. What they fail to realize is that sharing will bring more to everyone, including themselves.

The issue of ownership is an important one, because how you view ownership determines how you use your time and resources; how you use your time and resources reveals what is truly important to you.

When you apply the principle of God's ownership in everyday life, it changes your outlook entirely.

It is no longer "How do I want to spend my day?" It is now, "God, how do you want me to spend Your day?"

It is no longer, "How do I want to spend my money?" It is now, "God, how do you want me to spend Your money?"

It is no longer, "How much of my money do I want to give to the Lord?" It is now, "God, how much of Your money should I be keeping for myself?"

It is no longer, "How do I want to care for and feed my body?" It is now, "God, how do You want me to care for and feed Your body?"

It is no longer, "How do I want to raise my children?" It is now, "God, how do You want me to raise Your children?"

It is no longer, "What kind of house and car do I want to have?" It is now, "God, what kind of house and car do You want me to have?"

Getting back on the Go(l)d Standard means acknowledging that: God owns everything; I am His steward, called to manage His property faithfully; money should be used for relational purposes — first to love God, then to love people.

Just as it is today, gold in the Bible is a symbol of love. And not just any old love. Gold symbolizes higher loves than, say, love of food and drink or love of fresh air and sunshine — as good and wholesome as those loves are. As the most precious metal known in Bible times, gold represents the most precious kind of love.

What is the most precious love — from a spiritual perspective?

Gold, in the Bible, represents heavenly and spiritual love: the love of God and the love of our fellow human beings. These are the loves that Jesus tells us are central to human life.

Now, this love is not just a theoretical thing that we feel in our heart. If we truly love God and our fellow human beings, we will spend our lives doing good things for them. And even though we cannot do good things for God directly, Jesus tells us that if we do good things for others, we are doing good things for God.

So gold is not only a symbol of our love for God and our fellow human beings, it is also a symbol of all the good and thoughtful things we do for them out of love. Gold is mentioned in the second-to-last chapter of the Bible. Revelation 21:21 says that the streets of the heavenly city, new Jerusalem, are paved with pure gold. Translation: the streets of the city are paved with pure *love*, meaning that in God's kingdom, the roads we travel every day are pathways of love.

"I have held many things in my hands and lost them all, but whatever I have placed in God´s hands, that I still possess." – Martin Luther

Ownership – a true story

Enrique Hernandez (real name changed) collected many national awards as a renowned sportsman. But Enrique had a small secret. No one knew he was in deep financial trouble. His debt amounted to $900,000., which was eating up his business like a cancer.

He signed up for one of my financial seminars. At the end of the day, he went home shocked. He had never heard the Word of God applied to his life and his business in such a relevant way. He realized that he was not being a good manager of the blessings God entrusted to him. He decided that he was going to change the way he managed his business.

I met with him in a restaurant to probe for the spiritual roots of the problem. I asked Enrique about his assets and liabilities. He owned a very large empty building in the city, and it was fully paid for but completely empty. Enrique said that this was a very special building: for him it was the fulfilment of a dream. He explained that when he was a little boy, his family was extremely poor. He worked shining shoes, but he had big dreams! When cleaning the shoes of a rich businessman, he would say to himself, "Enrique, one day you too will have your own factory!" That huge building was the fulfillment of his dream.

There was only one problem. The building had been sitting empty for several years, and all of his attempts to start production in his factory had failed.

The next day at my seminar would be a life-changing experience for Enrique. The topic of the night was ownership and stewardship.

I explained that God owns it all. As the Bible says, *". . . You are not your own, for you were bought with a price. So glorify God . . ."* (1 Corinthians 6:19-20, ESV). Even though this may sound familiar, saying that God owns it all is much easier than living it and surrendering to God, trusting in His provision, and allowing Him to be in control.

This next sentence is another one that sounds easy but represents a huge victory in surrender: Emotional detachment to finances is a critical step to make in our journey to financial healing.

Enrique went home that night, prayed to the Lord, and realized that he had surrendered everything to the Lord except one thing: his dream. The emotional attachment to his dream was not allowing him to behave like an administrator of God's possessions.

Enrique surrendered to God what he considered the most precious possession he had in life: his childhood dream.

The following week, Enrique called a meeting with all of his creditors and explained to them that he owned a very large building. "The building is empty, and I am ready to sell it. It is valued at 1.1 million dollars. I am willing to give it to you in exchange for all my debts."

The creditors were surprised, but they accepted the exchange. Enrique was set free from the bondage of debt.

Later, he started a business again and became prosperous. He would say without reservation that the secret was the life-changing experience in realizing that he must behave each day as a trustee of God's possessions, acting as a manager in full recognition that God must be the absolute owner of everything – including his most cherished dreams.

Have you relinquished ownership and accepted a new assignment as the manager of what God gives you?

Directional pointer #1

The first directional pointer in navigating the journey of a financial disciple is to acknowledge, accept, and embrace God's ownership of all things, including "your" money. *"Yours, Lord, is the greatness and the power and the glory and the majesty and the splendor, for everything in heaven and earth is yours. Yours, Lord, is the kingdom; you are exalted as head over all. Wealth and honor come from you; you are the ruler of all things. In your hands are strength and power to exalt and give strength to all"* (1 Chronicles 29:11-12).

—

CHAPTER 30

—

Compass Point Northeast: The Power of Money

The power of money

Traveling from true north, we move eastward, focusing on God's values and following His instructions as we manage His resources. We reach the next compass point: the need to realize that hidden forces are seeking to tempt us off track.

It is very easy to say, "God owns it all," and decide to relinquish ownership; it is very difficult to live it out day by day. Most Christians have never been faced with a decision to renounce all they have, as Jesus posed it to the crowds in Luke 14:33. I believe this is a one-time major life decision we all must make. However, this decision is followed by daily obedience and devotion to God's way of handling money, just as baptism is a one-time event evidenced by daily following Jesus.

The great Reformer, Martin Luther, once wrote, "There are three conversions necessary: the conversion of the heart, the conversion of the mind, and the conversion of the purse. Of these three, it may well be that we find the conversion of the purse to be the most difficult." Charles Spurgeon wrote, "With some [Christians], the last part of their nature that ever gets sanctified is their wallet."

Money is power

Money is power. In itself, money is neutral — neither good nor bad. It is a medium of exchange. However, financial disciples must realize that Jesus unmasked a power behind money. In His Sermon on the Mount, He contrasts three sets of opposites: treasures on earth versus treasures in heaven, light versus darkness, and God versus money. If you were in the audience when Jesus spoke about two masters and said, "You cannot serve both God and (blank)," how would you expect Him to finish the sentence? I would expect "God and Satan" or even "God and Caesar" or "God and Baal." But Jesus rarely does the expected. His depth of understanding confounds expectations. I would be pushing rewind to see what I had missed.

When Jesus said, "You cannot be servants of God and of money," He is personifying money as a rival god. Jesus is emphasizing that money is more than just an impersonal medium of exchange. More than a simple resource to be used in good or bad ways depending on our attitude toward it, there is an elusive power behind money. It has godlike characteristics that pry you and me away from being servants of God to being its servants instead.

You don't think money is powerful? Why do we refer to money as purchasing power? Why do we attach symbols to money – prestige, status, glamour, even our sense of worth? Why do we refer to currency as the "Almighty Dollar?" Money in modern society is godlike, a substitute God. And if we aren't careful, it will rule and ruin our lives. Henry Fielding was right: "If you make money your god, it will plague you like the devil."

Managing money is a spiritual discipline. We must realize, as financial disciples, that managing our money, setting financial goals, is a spiritual discipline. It must be done prayerfully, with knowledge of God's financial principles, in prayer, led by the Holy Spirit, and in complete obedience to His Word.

How the power of money tempts us to get off track

Dan Schilling, my colleague at Compass, tells of his experience in teaching a series of webinars about the topic of greed. While researching the Scriptures, the Lord convicted him of how much greed still resided in his heart. Dan said, "While writing the material for this series, it was like looking into a steamed-up mirror. I kept wiping some parts off and started to see more and more of my heart, which revealed multiple elements of greed. It was very convicting but healthy to allow the Lord to draw my heart closer to him so I can be healed."

Pastor and writer Tim Keller, tells of the series of talks he gave to businesspeople about "The Seven Deadly Sins." He was pleasantly surprised at the level of attendance. When the day came for his talk on "Greed," his wife stopped him as he was heading out the door. "Tim, prepare for a low crowd today!" Sure enough, it was the least popular topic.

Jesus' Great Commission challenges us to "go and make disciples of all nations, baptizing them in the name of the Father and of the Son and of the Holy Spirit, and teaching them to obey everything I have commanded you" (Matthew 28:19-20). Instead of being baptized (fully immersed) in the Holy Trinity, money calls us to be baptized in the unholy trinity of I, me, and myself.

When struggling to come to spiritual maturity as financial disciples, we must be aware of the competition for our allegiance from within. The Bible calls this the flesh. "The desires of the flesh are against the Spirit, and the desires of the Spirit are against the flesh, for these are opposed to each other, to keep you from doing the things you want to do" (Galatians 5:17, ESV).

The Bible uses the term "the flesh" as a designation for indwelling sin, that part of us that remains opposed to the Lord and against which we struggle until we reach our heavenly home, completely free from the power and presence of sin.

Although possessions and money are not evil in themselves, John warns us, "Do not love the world or anything in the world. If anyone loves the world, love for the Father is not in them. For everything in the world – the lust of the flesh, the lust of the eyes, and the pride of life – comes not from the Father but from the world" (1 John 2:15). This challenges us to examine our motives when setting goals or making a major financial decision. The "things in the world" are not inherently evil or wrong to have. On the contrary, God "richly provides us with everything for our enjoyment" (1 Timothy 6:17). But enjoying things properly means not allowing them to become our master, to capture our love, to demand our devotion, to be the source of our hope.

Idolatry

Randy Alcorn states, "Idolatry is worshiping and serving anything other than the one true God. Everything material we have, including money, is either a tool or an idol. If we fail to use it as a tool for God's intended purposes, it mutates into an idol." The New Testament tells us that "greed . . . is idolatry" (Colossians 3:5).

This is exactly the power of money's tactic – to lead us to believe that something we can buy will fulfill desires and longings that only God can fulfill. The power of money leads us to focus on material things, which can never fully satisfy our longings. This focus ultimately leads us into all sorts of problems. "Those who want to get rich fall into temptation and a trap and into many foolish and harmful desires that plunge people into ruin and destruction. For the love of money is a root of all kinds of evil. Some people, eager for money, have wandered from the faith and pierced themselves with many griefs" (1 Timothy 6:9-10).

Idolatry can easily seem like a distant, abstract reality – something that takes place in Hollywood or Wall Street or Washington. We may vaguely recognize it in the shows and ads we see on our televisions, tablets, and phones. But we rarely sense its ugly presence in our own lives.

The great reformer, John Calvin stated, "From this we may gather that man's nature, so to speak, is a perpetual factory of idols. Man's mind, full as it is of pride and boldness, dares to imagine a god according to its own capacity; as it sluggishly plods, indeed is overwhelmed with the crassest ignorance, it conceives an unreality and an empty appearance as God." The psalmist says, "Those who make [idols] become like them, so do all who trust in them" (Psalm 135:18, ESV). We become what we worship!

The atheistic philosopher, Albert Camus stated, "Any life directed toward money is death." But fortunately, when we worship and serve the Lord, we find life. Financial disciples tear down the idols in their life and replace them with seeking the one true God daily.

How to break the power of money in our lives

Imagine stamping everything in your possession with the reminder "Given by God, owned by God, and to be used for the purposes of God." I have a silver Swiss five-franc coin. On the rim of the coin is written, "Dominus Providibit," – the Lord will provide. We need to find ways to remind ourselves over and over again that the earth is the Lord's, not ours, and that He provides what we need, not we ourselves.

How can we enjoy victory over the power of money that constantly tempts people to depart from God's ways? How can this power be disarmed so that we can be free to serve God and our fellow men with generous lives?

The best way to test counterfeit money is to use light. When shops or businesses are testing for it, they put it on a light box and let light shine through. And that's the way we can tell when the power of money and the lure of wealth is active in our lives. The more light we shine upon it – the more light from the Word of God we can shine upon our financial dealings and our financial decisions – the more we can tell if they are correct and in alignment with God's principles.

We need to test financial dealings, advice, and plans according to the light of the Bible, the light of the Word of God. I remember talking once to the head of the fraud squad of Scotland Yard in London. His area of expertise was discovering counterfeit money. I commented, "Sir, you must spend a lot of time studying all of these false bank notes."

"No, not at all," he replied. "I spend more time studying the real ones. So then I know when they deviate from the real thing."

That's what we need to do with our financial dealings. We need to spend a lot of time studying what the Bible says about how to handle our finances so we can understand how the power of money is tempting us to deviate from the real thing.

Giving is a winning strategy, a victory over the dark powers that seek to control and oppress us. The powers that energize money cannot abide that very unnatural and uneconomic of acts — giving. God receives the money given and brings it into His economy. Then from His storehouse, He supplies.

An example of this is giving to the poor. "Whoever is kind to the poor lends to the Lord, and he will reward them for what they have done" (Proverbs 19:17).

The rich young ruler did not understand this. When asked by Jesus to sell everything and give it to the poor, he went away sad because he was very rich. He missed Jesus' offer of eternal life. He didn't realize that giving to the poor was lending to the Lord, who would, in some shape or form, repay the loan.

Giving a portion of our money to the Lord's work somehow sanctifies the whole. The power of money now works for you like yeast works in bread. The money we give to the Lord has the power to spread through our whole life. The Holy Spirit can then use the power of money to enhance God's work — not only for the recipient of the gift, but also for the giver. As the old Indian proverb says, "The hand that washes will itself become clean."

We need to depart from a lifestyle centered on money and possessions to practice a lifestyle of simplicity. A good starting point is to answer the question for yourself, "How much is enough?" How much is enough for my current responsibilities in the economic strata God has called me?

The pulling power of our desire for more is strong — the very thing we think will give us freedom ultimately leads us into captivity. This thought was captured succinctly by E.F. Schmacher in his seminal book Small is Beautiful. He states, "The cultivation and expansion of needs is the antithesis of wisdom. It is also the antithesis of freedom and peace. Every increase of needs tends to increase one's dependence on outside forces over which one cannot have control, and therefore increases existential fear. Only by a reduction of needs can one promote a genuine reduction in those tensions which are the ultimate causes of strife and war."

Essential to navigating the journey of a financial disciple is to realize that we have a strong, clever but very corrupt competitor – the power of money – constantly tempting us to steer off course. Financial disciples need to watch carefully for money's influence and embrace the victory Christ has provided for us.

Money is powerful. It is so powerful, taught Jesus, that it competes head-on for our devotion.

Overcoming this competition and the downward spiral of consumerism, materialism, and discontent is to grow in generosity. Jesus explained it very simply: you are more blessed when you give than when you receive.

PART 4: NAVIGATING THE JOURNEY
OF A FINANCIAL DISCIPLE

—

CHAPTER 31

—

Compass Point East: Financial Decisions

"Begin with the end in mind" is one of the principles in Stephen Covey's bestseller *The 7 Habits of Highly Effective People*. In its most basic form, it refers to always having the image of the end of your life as your frame of reference to evaluate everything else. The best decisions are those taken in the light of their eternal impact.

The great reformer Martin Luther said, "There are only two days on my calendar. Today and that day!" Of course, he was referring to the great day of Christ's return. He constantly taught people to look at what they do *today* in the light of *that day*. We should learn to make every decision today in the light of eternity. What effect will my decision today have on eternity?

Making the right financial decisions means following Jesus when He said, *"Do not lay up for yourselves treasures on earth, where moth and rust destroy and where thieves break in and steal, but lay up for yourselves treasures in heaven, where neither moth nor rust destroys and where thieves do not break in and steal. For where your treasure is, there your heart will be also"* (Matthew 6:19-21, ESV).

An important principle in making financial decisions is that where you put your money, your heart will follow. I know when you are investing in stocks and shares, your attention, your interest, your time is directed to following the progress of your investments. I found myself watching the market rates with unhealthy regularity!

Also, if you want to have a heart for evangelism or missions – start investing in evangelism and mission work! Your heart follows your money! Conversely, if your financial decisions are directed toward consumer goods, then you will develop a consumer mindset!

Getting directions from the Owner

To make the right financial decisions, we need to get directions from the Owner.

If we want to really discover what our Owner wants us to do with all that He has entrusted to us to manage for Him, we need to spend time in His Book. This should be so obvious that we should never need to mention it.

First, we need to be readers of His Word. Spending time reading the Owner's Manual is really far more a matter of having the *desire* to read it than having the *time* to read it. Starting to read the Bible on a daily basis is really more about a heart change than it is a schedule change.

Second, we need to study the Word, to dig deep and become students of the Word. We should be like the Bereans, who *"were of more noble character than those in Thessalonica, for they received the message with great eagerness and examined the Scriptures every day to see if what Paul said was true"* (Acts 17:11). They weren't just reading the Scriptures; they were studying them.

Third, we need to memorize Scripture, so that we always have God's Word ready at all times. David expresses this very idea in Psalm 119:11 (NASB), *"Your word I have treasured in my heart, that I may not sin against You."*

How we make decisions

When considering our financial decisions, we first need to consider how we make them. Our decisions are based on what we think and believe. Neil Anderson says, "All behavior is the product of what we choose to think or believe. . . . Trying to change behavior, without changing what we believe and therefore think, will never produce any lasting results."

So, we need to look at our beliefs. That is why we need to be students of the Word and indeed memorizers of the Word, so that God's Word can develop our beliefs and mold our thinking, which will determine our choices and behavior.

Our beliefs form our worldview – the way we look at the world – and determine our behavior. Our behavior determines outcomes and the subsequent choices we make to fix the outcomes we don't like. Here is an example.

If my belief is that I should spend "because I'm worth it," I will live for today, want to keep up with friends, and spend freely. My identity will be determined by my possessions. My thinking is to go with the flow and do as everyone else is doing. My behavior is that I spend too much, have no budget, don't know where the money goes, and have no rational criteria for making financial decisions. I then attempt to fix this by spending less money, trying to live on a budget, and starting to track my spending.

However, because of my beliefs, my outcome will be that I am out of money, constantly in debt, living from month to month, unable to save, and experiencing friction over money with my spouse. This results in fear of the future, a very uncomfortable state of affairs. I may try to escape from reality or I may try to fix the situation by deciding to borrow more, ask relatives for money, or even cheat.

The correct way of making financial decisions is to allow our thinking to be determined, not by what everyone else does, but by allowing God to transform our thinking. Romans 12:2 (NLT) says, *"Don't copy the behaviors and customs of this world, but let God transform you into a new person by changing the way you think."* Then our decisions will be based on what God wants us to do and the results will be good and pleasing to Him.

Making the right financial decisions starts with setting goals
It is vitally important to know where you are headed. Imagine a sprinter preparing to run a hundred-meter race. When the gun fires, all of the runners dash for the finish line except one. He runs hard but without direction, not knowing where the tape is. We can't imagine an athlete being so foolish. After all, the placement of the finish line determines everything about the race. Yet many of us run our financial lives without any idea of where our finish lines are. Lacking clearly defined goals, the years pass without the type of meaningful progress we desire because we don't know what we are trying to accomplish.

Without goals, our financial decisions are dictated by other people, unchecked emotions, and perceived urgency – all of which obstruct wise decision making. Most of us are satisfied with simply accumulating as much as we can, which is the world's way of thinking. Since the longing for more is insatiable, we never experience rest or financial freedom. When we choose to set financial objectives, our choices become purposeful, and we stay focused on what is most important.

A study of Harvard students revealed that three percent had written goals and plans. Thirteen percent had goals but no written plans, and eighty-seven percent had neither. Ten years later, the study showed that the thirteen percent who had goals were earning twice as much as those with no goals. But the three percent who had both goals and written plans were earning ten times as much.

Setting financial goals is so vitally important because:

1. Goal setting is the beginning of meaningful life planning. Until you have this, you have not started to plan your life.

2. A goal is not a goal until it is measurable; it is at best a good intention.

3. Only a Christian has the ability to set faith goals and ask, "God, what do you want me to achieve?" This is a way to experience the hand of God in my financial situation.

A Christian is in a privileged position to set faith goals. A faith goal is a statement: "I believe that God is leading me to _____."

Goals give direction and purpose. They help crystalize thinking. Goals provide personal motivation, and God will direct your steps. *"The heart of man plans his way, but the Lord establishes his steps"* (Proverbs 16:9, ESV). The faith process is: my goal setting comes from God, I seek His will and wisdom, I start to move, and He can direct my steps.

Biblical process for decision making

As we have been learning, the Bible is our source of wisdom and inspiration as we seek to make the right financial decisions. We can test our financial decisions according to these six "P" tests.

1. Prayer test
    Start by asking the Lord to reveal His pans so that you can align yourself with them. *"Call to me and I will answer you and tell you great and unsearchable things you do not know"* (Jeremiah 33:3).

2. Promise test
    Wisdom – knowing how, what, why, and when – is freely available to all who ask. *"If any of you lacks wisdom, you should ask God, who gives generously to all"* (James 1:5).

3. Partner test
    Getting advice and counsel from trusted partners will increase your ability to make the right decisions. *"A man of understanding will acquire wise counsel"* (Proverbs 1:5, NASB).

4. Purpose test
    When making financial decisions, are your motivations right? *". . . whatever you do, do it all for the glory of God"* (1 Corinthians 10:31).

5. Preference test
    You have a lot of freedom to make choices, and you can trust in the Lord to put the right desires in your heart! *"Delight yourself in the Lord, and He will give you the desires of your heart"* (Psalm 37:4, ESV).

6. Peace test
    Do you have peace about a financial decision? A lack of peace can be an indicator that you are not making the right choice. *"Let the peace of Christ rule in your hearts"* (Colossians 3:15).

Directional pointer #3

The third directional pointer in navigating the journey of a financial disciple is to prayerfully seek God's best, get godly counsel, and then follow the process – setting faith goals according to His revelation.

CHAPTER 32

—

Compass Point Southeast: Free from Debt

The origins of debt

When Eve was tempted by the serpent and had to give an account of what she had done, she explained, *"The serpent deceived me, and I ate"* (Genesis 3:13b). The word "deceived" in Hebrew comes from a root *"nasha,"* which is a homonym – a word having more than one basic meaning. It means both to deceive and to lend at interest. This Hebrew word is strongly linked to *"nashak,"* which means to strike with a sting.

The word appears in Habakkuk 2:7 (NIV). *"Will not your creditors [nashak] suddenly arise? Will they not wake up and make you tremble? Then you will become their prey."* This tells us that lending at interest is at its root a deceit, tempting people into bondage. Just like the serpent tempted Eve into a bargain of debt that she could never repay.

Borrowing money is almost like opening a Pandora's Box, because we never know what is going to happen next. Borrowing is trusting that in the future I will be able to repay. We do not know what the future will be like, and we have no control over future circumstances. Opening Pandora's Box refers to getting into a situation over which one has very little control.

According to the old Greek myth, Pandora was to be the first of a race of women, the first bride who would live with mortal men as companions – only in times of plenty – and desert them when times became difficult. Hmm, does this sound like a bank?

Pandora was actually sent as a curse to Zeus's men. She was given a present upon her marriage, a box that she was told never to open. Needless to say, her curiosity got the better of her (like eating forbidden fruit), and she unleashed eight demons into the world. The first seven were the seven deadly sins, and the last, which she managed to capture, was hope.

Debt removes freedom

The Bible says, *"The rich rule over the poor, and the borrower is slave to the lender"* (Proverbs 22:7). Debt removes our freedom, because our creditors gain the priority call on our finances; they have to be paid first. If we don't pay them first, they take steps to enforce their priority. Paul said, *"All things are lawful for me, but not all things are helpful. All things are lawful for me, but I will not be dominated by anything"* (1 Corinthians 6:12, ESV). Borrowing is not forbidden in the Bible, but it's always discouraged because we become dominated by it and it removes our freedom.

God wants us to remain free. *"For freedom Christ has set us free; stand firm therefore, and do not submit again to a yoke of slavery"* (Galatians 5:1, ESV). The source of our freedom is knowing the truth about what God has to say in the Bible about money. Jesus said, *". . . If you abide in my word, you are truly my disciples, and you will know the truth, and the truth will set you free"* (John 8:31-32, ESV).

God wants us to be able to love and honor others. In a chapter with significant references to money, Paul said, *"Pay to all what is owed to them: taxes to whom taxes are owed, revenue to whom revenue is owed, respect to whom respect is owed, honor to whom honor is owed. Owe no one anything, except to love each other, for the one who loves another has fulfilled the law"* (Romans 13:7-8, ESV).

If we do not pay our debts back on time, tension begins to build. The one we owe begins to wonder what kind of person we are. The relationship comes under stress and strain, and the first thing to go out the window is love; it gets replaced by a hostile creditor-versus-debtor relationship. It is very difficult to love our neighbor if we owe money that we cannot repay in full on time; the relationship starts to break down.

Being anxious about paying back our loans and credit can lead to denial, fear, isolation, ill health, despair, and relationship breakdown. Freedom from this kind of anxiety results in reduced stress and related illnesses, fewer family breakups, and even saved lives, because stress can be a killer. This freedom enables people to give generously, order their finances based on their chosen priorities, and work on life goals.

Debt also removes our flexibility to adapt to unexpected circumstances. Debt reduces our options, sometimes leaving only the most unpleasant.

And it makes us less able to respond to God's call to do something different, including serving those in need.

Why borrow?

Will Smith quipped, "We buy things we don't need with money we don't have to impress people we don't like." It is very important to question our motives for borrowing.

Professor Dr. Tomas Sedlacek, author of *The Economics of Good and Evil,* said, "Eve and Adam grab the opportunity and eat the fruit. The original sin has the character of excessive, unnecessary consumption. It is not of a sexual nature. A desire for something she doesn't need is awakened in Eve. The living conditions in paradise were complete, and yet everything God had given the two wasn't enough. In this sense, greed isn't just at the birthplace of theoretical economics, but also at the beginning of our history. Greed is the beginning of everything."

Why borrow? The root of the answer is exposed in an honest searching of our motives. Is it greed, the desire for more? If so, pursuing it will never satisfy. *"He who loves money will not be satisfied with money, nor he who loves wealth with his income; this also is vanity"* (Ecclesiastes 5:10, ESV).

Before deciding on a major decision to borrow, it is good to pray and seek God's wisdom. *"Search me, O God, and know my heart! Try me and know my thoughts! And see if there be any grievous way in me, and lead me in the way everlasting!* (Psalm 139:23-24, ESV).

We should borrow only for projects that promote human flourishing. Examples could be home ownership, a college education, starting a business, or essentials for work. Consumer borrowing is always economically bad. Wait, save, and pay cash!

If borrowing is necessary, follow these three rules: (1) The economic return must be greater than the economic cost; (2) I must have a guaranteed way to repay; (3) my spouse must be in agreement.

Biblical danger warnings

The future is uncertain. When borrowing, am I presuming on God to provide? There is no reason to believe that God will provide in this case. I am trusting that future circumstances will put me in a position to make my payments. They may not, and God has not obligated Himself to provide for my presumption. Is it not better to wait until God provides in the present and then make the purchase?

"Come now, you who say, 'Today or tomorrow we will go into such and such a town and spend a year there and trade and make a profit' – yet you do not know what tomorrow will bring. What is your life? For you are a mist that appears for a little time and then vanishes. Instead you ought to say, 'If the Lord wills, we will live and do this or that.' As it is, you boast in your arrogance. All such boasting is evil. So whoever knows the right thing to do and fails to do it, for him it is sin" (James 4:13-17, ESV).

Giving in to temptation leads us into problematic economic and personal situations. Debt is mammon's slippery banana peel! We enjoy the fruit without realizing that the peel in which it was wrapped will trip us up. *"But those who desire to be rich fall into temptation, into a snare, into many senseless and harmful desires that plunge people into ruin and destruction"* (1 Timothy 6:9, ESV).

Borrowing can cause us to miss God's provision. Am I denying God an opportunity to work? Who is my provider, the bank or God? *"Keep your life free from love of money, and be content with what you have, for he has said, 'I will never leave you nor forsake you.' So we can confidently say, 'The Lord is my helper; I will not fear; what can man do to me?'"* (Hebrews 13:5-6, ESV).

The obligation of debt can tie us down and remove our availability for the Lord to direct our path. *"So therefore, any one of you who does not renounce all that he has cannot be my disciple"* (Luke 14:33, ESV).

We should avoid personally guaranteeing loans. Solomon, in the book of Proverbs, gives many warnings such as, *"Be not one of those who give pledges, who put up security for debts. If you have nothing with which to pay, why should your bed be taken from under you?"* (Proverbs 22:26-27, ESV).

Before entering any credit situation, we should get counsel. First, from God's Word, then from our spouse, and finally from godly people. *"Listen to advice and accept instruction, that you may gain wisdom in the future"* (Proverbs 19:20, ESV).

Paying back loans

Paying back is a minimum requirement to live a godly life. *"The wicked borrows but does not pay back, but the righteous is generous and gives"* (Psalm 37:21, ESV). The word "wicked" means being hostile to God, being morally wrong. We certainly don't want to be in that state! Not paying on time dishonors God. *"You shall not steal; you shall not deal falsely; you shall not lie to one another. You shall not swear by my name falsely, and so profane the name of your God: I am the Lord"* (Leviticus 19:11-12, ESV).

Paying back on time and in full is loving your neighbor as yourself. *"Do not withhold good from those to whom it is due, when it is in your power to do it. Do not say to your neighbor, 'Go, and come again, tomorrow I will give it' – when you have it with you. Do not plan evil against your neighbor, who dwells trustingly beside you"* (Proverbs 3:27-29, ESV).

Directional pointer #4

The fourth directional pointer in navigating the journey of a financial disciple is to become debt free, ensuring maximum freedom and flexibility to respond to any need. Being free from debt ensures us of better chances to survive, to do God's work, and to flourish through difficult times.

PART 4: NAVIGATING THE JOURNEY
OF A FINANCIAL DISCIPLE

—

CHAPTER 33

—

Compass Point South: How Much is Enough?

How much is enough? This is a very easy question to ask but a difficult question to answer. Finding the correct answer, however, brings the opportunity to realize the most important values in our lives. A simple but true answer to the question is this: God will always give you enough to do His will. He always pays for what He orders.

"And God is able to make all grace abound to you, so that having all sufficiency in all things at all times, you may abound in every good work" (2 Corinthians 9:8, ESV).

God's grace is given to us so that we have sufficient supply for our needs – enough to live a godly, joyful life – and enough to do good things and be generous.

I recently read a short article from a young professional, Renate Rijsberg. She says, "In recent weeks I discussed the issue of finances with people around me. During a dinner with family, at work, and in a relaxed evening with friends, I asked a few questions, kept my ears open and noticed what people had to say.

"First of all, I was amazed at the taboo hanging around the topic of money. It is always a bit vague. Telling your salary is "not-done," the state of your bank account is very private. We only tell others when we have made a bargain buy or bought a mega-expensive product. And truth be known, I feel the same. The more I earn, the more I need to make ends meet. You constantly strive to earn more, to give your family more, taking a vacation at least twice a year, live in a beautiful house with a large garden, ride a nice car, have enough savings in the bank and, if possible, share with everyone.

"Money is playing such a huge role in our society that it seems like you don't count any more if you don't have 'enough' money. And even if you do have all the things I just mentioned, then the question remains if all this satisfies you."

The Greek philosopher Epicurus answered our "How much is enough?" question this way: "Nothing is enough for the man to whom enough is too little."

Contrast that with the well-known answer from J.D. Rockefeller. When the multi-millionaire was asked "How much is enough?" he answered, "Just a little bit more." He may have said it over a hundred years ago, but it seems to characterize today's capitalist system.

The problems with overconsumption

The problem of not having a satisfactory answer to our question was tackled by Professor Dr. Thomas Sedlacek in his book, *The Economics of Good and Evil.* "The more we have, the more we want. Why? Perhaps we thought (and this sounds truly intuitive) that the more we have, the less we will need. We thought that consumption leads to saturation of our needs. But the opposite has proven to be true. The more we have, the more additional things we need. Every new satisfied want will beget a new one and will leave us wanting. For consumption is like a drug."

If the question of enough is not settled, we will always be left wanting. According to Sedlacek, we become victims to "affluenza," the sickness of our times for which the cure is the answer to our question.

Anselm Grün is a Benedictine monk and director of a large group of enterprises that employ over 600 people in southern Germany. He leads these enterprises according to Franciscan rules, and in his 2015 book, *Of Greed and Desire,* he agrees with Sedlacek, arguing that the attitude of never having enough leads to a very unrestful behavior, "a nomadic existence," and continual dissatisfaction. "When we desire possessions, we are looking for rest which we never find because we ultimately discover that the possessions are possessing us and lead us into more needs."

Listening to Sedlacek and Grün, we can conclude that the answer lies in our ability to limit our needs and desires, to develop a sober lifestyle of sufficiency in which we can be content and thankful for all God has given us to enjoy. If we do not pursue such a path, we become subject to inward desires and outside forces that control us, resulting in loss of freedom.

I fear that we are all either trapped or on our way to being trapped by the lure of more; it seems like we are constantly heading for a black hole.

Looking at the sociological and psychological consequences of our all-consuming epidemic, psychologists Tim Kasser and Robert Putman argue, "It's a particular strand of overconsumption, where we purchase things, not to fulfill our basic needs, but where we use stuff to fill some voids about our lives and make social statements about ourselves. Our obsessive relationship with material things is actually jeopardizing our relationships, which have proven over and over to be the biggest determining factor in our happiness once our basic needs are met.

"Beyond a minimum threshold of poverty, money doesn't buy happiness. Wealth may seem like a solution to your problems, but often it simply replaces the ones it solves. As paychecks increase, lifestyles usually match those increases. This results in the same financial worries and budgeting problems, just with more stuff. A preoccupation with owning things is a poor attempt to fill a vacuum. Occasionally stuff can fill that vacuum. Buying that new computer or fancy car might temporarily shrink the hole. But quickly you adapt to the new upgrades and the hole grows, enslaving you to earn higher and higher paychecks with no way out."

Answering the question, "How much is enough?" can be an antidote to overconsumption; thinking and meditating on this question can lead us to consider what "enough" means for each of us personally.

If we determine the threshold of enough, any income over and above that can be utilized to build assets to invest in doing good – first of all to our family and friends and then to the world at large.

It is great to reach the place where we can say, "This is enough." This place can be reached sooner then we think. Paul wrote to Timothy, *"But if we have food and clothing, we will be content with that"* (1 Timothy 6:8). John the Baptist said to some curious Roman soldiers, *". . . be content with your pay"* (Luke 3:14).

Little-known Agur, a writer of proverbs in the Bible, wrote a wonderful prayer. *"Give me neither poverty nor riches; feed me with the food that is needful for me, lest I be full and deny you and say, 'Who is the Lord?' or lest I be poor and steal and profane the name of my God"* (Proverbs 30:8-9, ESV).

He is basically asking God to reveal to him what is *"needful"* for him. That, then, will be enough for him. Agur says that if he has more, he might think he doesn't need God anymore. On the other hand, Agur says to God that if he does not have enough, he may be tempted to cut corners and find dishonest ways of getting what he needs.

It should be a matter of prayer to determine the balance between the two extremes. Riches are more than enough, and poverty is not having enough. One may lead to dependency on money and possessions and independence from God. The other can lead to behavior that does not honor God: lying, cheating, stealing.

Can you earnestly pray, as Jesus taught us, "Give me today my daily bread"? That is, "Lord please provide enough for what I need for life." I have learned to live on "enough" for many years. Sometimes I have had more and been able to bless others with it; but I have never been let down by God and not had enough!

A spending plan can help you answer the question for yourself. Consider making a new plan with your partner. In prayer, ask God, "How much is enough for my situation and responsibilities?"

I believe we all should seek to see what we can do without. *"But whatever gain I had, I counted as loss for the sake of Christ. Indeed, I count everything as loss because of the surpassing worth of knowing Christ Jesus my Lord"* (Philippians 3:7-8, ESV).

Contentment

A sense of contentment is a prerequisite for properly answering the "How much is enough?" question. But it is also a fruit of properly answering it, because contentment is not the fulfillment of our wants; it is appreciation for what God has given us and the freedom to share it with others.

Mother Theresa is quoted as saying, "Once the longing for money comes, the longing also comes for what money can give: superfluities, nice rooms, luxuries at table, more clothes, and so on. Our needs will increase, for one thing brings another, and the result will be endless dissatisfaction."

Is financial contentment really possible in today's society? We seem to be bombarded with limitless options in a society where we are constantly told we will never be happy unless we have the latest innovation, the newest technology, the biggest-screen TV. I want to get off this merry-go-round and find true contentment. To be satisfied with my circumstances, not complaining, not craving something else, and having a mind at peace.

I have learned that contentment has nothing to do with money. It's a learned response, a deliberately chosen attitude.

The apostle Paul taught this very clearly: *"I am not saying this because I am in need, for I have learned to be content whatever the circumstances. I know what it is to be in need, and I know what it is to have plenty. I have learned the secret of being content in any and every situation, whether well fed or hungry, whether living in plenty or in want"* (Philippians 4:11-12).

How can we achieve this state of contentment that is independent of circumstances? The answer was given by Paul in Philippians 4:13 (NLT),

"I can do everything through Christ, who gives me strength." I like what Major Ian Thomas, founder of the Torchbearers ministry, says: "All you need is what you have; what you have is what He is; you cannot have more; and you do not need to have less."

No financial principle can have a greater impact on you or free you up more than this truth: Money is not the key to contentment! Contentment has everything to do with your relationship with God and nothing to do with your money. Once you are free from the love of money and the pursuit of it, you can have a lot or a little and be content all the same. At that point you have learned the secret of contentment.

A long-term perspective on wealth creation

Leo Tolstoy tells the story of a greedy man named *Pahom*, who was obsessed by amassing more and more land. One day he learned of a wonderful and unusual opportunity to get still more land. For only 1,000 rubles he could have the entire area he could walk around in a day, but he had to make it back to the starting point by sunset or he would lose everything he invested.

He arose early and set out. He walked on and on, thinking that he could get just a little more land if he kept straining forward for the prize he sought. But he went so far that he realized he must walk very fast if he was going to get back to the starting point and claim the land. As the sun set lower in the sky, he quickened his pace. He began to run. He came within sight of his starting point and exerted his last burst of energy. Plunging over the finish line, he fell to the ground. Dead.

His servant took a spade and dug a grave. He made it just long enough and just wide enough to match *Pahom's* body and buried him. Here's the title Tolstoy gave his story: *How Much Land Does a Man Need?*

He ends this short story with this line: "Six feet from his head to his heels was all that man needed."

Directional pointer #5

The fifth directional pointer in navigating the journey of a financial disciple is to answer the question, "How Much Is Enough?" How much is enough to do all the Lord is asking me to do? Should the Lord provide above and beyond "enough," the financial disciple can be ready with a faith plan to use the surplus for Kingdom purposes.

CHAPTER 34

—

Compass Point Southwest: Whole-life Prosperity

Our culture trains us to think that wealth typically refers only to financial assets and worldly possessions. But a moment's reflection shows that a well-lived life (we could call it *true* wealth) is about much more than finances.

For example, if you become a millionaire but lose all your friends and family, are you wealthy? Is that a good trade-off? Is that a well-lived life? Is it worth losing friends to get more money? If you make more money than everyone else in the world but live in a house by yourself all day with an incurable illness that gives you chronic pain, are you wealthy? Is that a good life? How much money is chronic pain worth? Would you rather have a rich teacher or a wise teacher?

I think most of us would agree that a life isn't good if it's filled with financial prosperity but no other kind of well-being.

Our problem, then, is that our measurement of wealth is too narrow. We need to expand our definition of what kind of return on our investments we're looking for. We need to think much wider about prosperity and wealth.

In 3 John 2, the apostle John prays that the recipient of the letter would prosper in *"all respects"* and that he would be in good health, *"just as your soul prospers."* The writer is giving us a holistic view of prosperity that is a helpful corrective against the short-sighted focus of the so-called prosperity gospel. John is saying that *every area of your life should prosper*, not just one or two. He describes prosperity in terms of multiple kinds of capital and currency.

This way of looking at prosperity helps keep everything in proper orientation and guards us against the excesses of a narrow focus on only one area of capital to the detriment of the others. The problem with prosperity theology is that it is narrowly focused on measuring financial prosperity when it ought to be thinking about spiritual, relational, physical, and productive prosperity too. It follows the way of the world in valuing financial capital above all else instead of recognizing financial capital in its proper biblical place. We tend to think of financial capital as the ceiling when it's actually only the floor.

Life wealth

Here is a good, integrated definition of life wealth.

Life wealth is the accumulation of financial, relational, physical, productive, and spiritual capital with which we can achieve our God-given goals.

Focusing on developing, managing, and growing these five capitals will bring balance to these five dimensions of wealth that are accessible to each one of us. Here are the five capitals we see revealed in Scripture, listed from lowest to highest in value.

1. Financial capital: Your money, assets, and material possessions.

2. Physical capital: Your physical well-being, health, wellness, fitness, rest, and recreation.

3. Productive capital: Your personal proficiencies, gifting, skills, IQ, and attitudes plus your formal education. It embraces learning, skill development, and unique abilities and talents.

4. Relational capital: All relationships with the people in your life; parents, siblings, extended family, friends, co-workers, teachers, neighbors, and acquaintances.

5. Spiritual capital: The place God and faith occupy in your life.

Financial capital

We are most familiar with this one because we work with it every day. Neither good nor bad, it's simply a resource we have available to use. Financial capital is the money and possessions we have to invest.

The resources of financial capital to invest are denominated in euros, dollars, pesos, etc.

When we think financial capital is the most important, we are willing to sacrifice all kinds of other capital to get it. Working late at the office might get us a great bonus at the end of the year, but in doing so we sacrifice relational capital with our children, who wish we were home to read a story and tuck them in at night. We also sacrifice our physical capital, as our health begins to fail from overwork. We sacrifice spiritual capital because we don't attend to our relationship with Jesus sufficiently – or at all – for some time. Eventually, life stops working properly because we've made a foolish investment, sacrificing capital that was more valuable (spiritual, relational, physical) to grow capital that was less valuable (financial).

Physical capital

This is the time and energy we have available to invest. It comprises the time we make available for tasks, projects, and relationships as well as the capacity we have to use that time effectively. The resources to invest are hours and energy.

Jesus shows us how to do this when he teaches his disciples how to rest and abide so they can bear fruit. Read Matthew 11:28-30 and John 15:5.

Getting proper rest and living in a rhythm of life that allows us to work hard *and* play hard is essential if we are going to steward our long-term physical capital.

We develop physical capital by properly allocating time for our priorities in keeping with the energy we have available. Our overall health is very relevant, because it greatly affects our ability to invest our time and energy. If we're sick, we can't work (financial and productive capital). Likewise, if we have a migraine, we can't deliver a lecture or write a book (productive capital). We can't solve a problem in a brainstorming meeting if we're home ill.

Productive capital

This is the creativity and knowledge we have available to invest and make things happen. It is of higher value than financial capital, because we can't create ideas and creativity, get things done, or produce anything simply by spending a lot of money. Productive capital is accumulated through creativity, know-how, learning, and doing. The resources to invest are ability, skills, concepts, and ideas.

Jesus possessed an astonishing level of productive capital, which He used often in His mission. In the culture of His day, Jesus was recognized by the crowds, His disciples, and even His enemies as a Rabbi, which means "teacher" or "master." Jesus wasn't just a holy person who prayed a lot – He was also a smart person who thought a lot. As Dallas Willard has said, "Jesus wasn't just nice, he was brilliant!"

Jesus also got things done well! "And they were astonished beyond measure, saying, *"He has done all things well"* (Mark 7:37, ESV).

The CEO of a large company said, "Customers will not pay you for your education or experience, for how much you know, but for how useful your knowledge is in helping them achieve their goals."

Remember, people don't care how much you know (productive capital) until they know how much you care (relational capital).

Spending productive capital in the right way requires wisdom, an integration of knowledge, skills, talents, gifts, experience, and understanding.

Relational capital

This is the "relational wealth" we have available to invest, measured in family and friends, the quantity and quality of our relationships with others. Relational capital is concerned with how much relational wealth we have to invest. The resources to invest are family, friends, and co-workers.

We see Jesus invest his physical capital to grow his relational capital with his disciples. In fact, none of the other capitals can actually grow without a relationship of some kind. Jesus invested quite a bit of time in just a few disciples, deepening his relational capital with them because he knew they would need it for the "job" he was going to give them.

Relational capital is more valuable than financial, physical, and productive capital because you really can't do anything of value in life without a relationship with someone where there is a good level of mutual trust. In essence, you can't really do anything with your financial, physical, or productive capital unless you have relational capital.

Jesus grew his relational capital by investing his physical capital in his covenantal relationships. The covenantal relationship Jesus forged with his disciples formed the basis of the Kingdom breakthrough he was able to achieve through them.

Spiritual capital

This is the "spiritual equity" we have available to invest, measured in authority and power. We see people astonished at Jesus' teaching because it was filled with authority and wisdom. His miracles expressed a degree of God's power that they had never seen before. Jesus was "rich" in spiritual capital, which gave Him the resources necessary to carry out His mission – opening up the doors of the Kingdom of God to everyone. We see Jesus constantly urging people to trade in other forms of capital to gain this one.

For Jesus, this is the ultimate payoff of living as His disciple: you grow your spiritual capital, which has the highest value of all the capitals. When Jesus talked about life in the Kingdom of God and how it was worth cashing in everything else for it, He was talking about a life rich in spiritual capital. When Jesus talked about eternal life, He wasn't just talking about long-lasting life – he was talking about a life rich in spiritual capital that lasts forever. The Kingdom of God and eternal life are like code words to refer to a life filled with spiritual capital.

Think about another economic metaphor Jesus used. He said that a relationship with Him and with the Father through Him, is like finding a pearl of *"great price,"* which far exceeded the value of anything else. It's like finding a treasure in a field. If you find a treasure of great worth in a field, the smart thing to do is liquidate everything so you can buy the field. That's Jesus' message to us about the value of spiritual capital – it's far more valuable than your money, so you will do well to sell everything to get it. Cash it all in for that one thing that is most valuable. It just makes good economic sense!

Directional pointer #6

The sixth directional pointer in navigating the journey of a financial disciple is to build whole-life prosperity, keeping a good balance between financial, physical, relational, productive, and spiritual prosperity.

CHAPTER 35

—

Compass Point West: Generosity

Whole-life generosity – sharing time, talents, treasure, and the gospel – is the lifestyle outcome of a financial disciple.

It begins by realizing a kind of generosity cycle. This starts with a realization that all of our life is lived in relationship to God and is centered around the cross of Christ, who loved us and gave His life for us. When we realize that He spent His life to set us free and that everything we have is a gift from God, it gives rise to deep gratitude.

Out of thankfulness for what God has done for us, we then want to release all we have for the blessing of others. So, whole-life generosity is an overflowing life that is released to God for the blessing of others.

Whole-life generosity begins by acknowledging our sinful, self-centered nature and accepting Christ's offer of transformation. Then we consciously decide to choose God's eternal Kingdom over earthly desires. Finally, as we become conformed to the image of Christ, we become sacrificial givers who reflect Jesus' generosity. It is said you are never more like Christ than when you are giving. It is interesting that Gandhi, probably one of the most influential people of his day, said this, "Oh, I don't reject Christ. I love Christ. It's just that so many of you Christians are so unlike Christ. If Christians would really live according to the teachings of Christ as found in the Bible, all of India would be Christian today."

Drawn into the day-to-day concerns, absorbed and even sometimes drowning in our own routines, we forget that each breath we take is God's gift to us. Yet when we open our eyes and hearts, we realize that we have been blessed so that we can be a blessing to others. Live the generous life. Give radically. Share your blessings.

Planning your giving

Our goal should be to release abundance. Giving starts with God's provision – we give because He first gives to us! *"But who am I, and who are my people, that we should be able to give as generously as this? Everything comes from you, and we have given you only what comes from your hand"* (1 Chronicles 29:14). The gifts which the people brought for the building of the temple were abundant. David realized that we are merely channels of God's gifts.

In planning our giving, it is important to start with prayerful and responsible spending. The extent of our expenditures must be limited by answering the question: "How much is enough for the lifestyle I believe God would want for me, given the responsibilities I have?"

God will only bless us with abundance and allow us to enjoy overflow when we limit our lifestyle. He will not pour money into a bucket with holes in it!

This means we have to decrease our borrowing, plan for paying our taxes in full and on time, plan for future needs, and plan our giving. Then we can begin to experience God's promise, *"And God is able to make all grace abound to you, so that having all sufficiency in all things at all times, you may abound in every good work"* (2 Corinthians 9:8. ESV).

As God grants abundance, we can grow in generosity beyond what we would think possible and experience the cycle of giving and receiving in faith. We cannot out-give God! He will always give us more to give.

Planned giving is not only for those with high or medium incomes. There is a wonderful example from India called "A handful of rice." Called to serve God from the corner of their kitchens where no one but God sees their generosity, the poor women of Mizoram in north-eastern India have created a culture of generational generosity — for more than a hundred years.

Described as a revolution, these women, no matter how little they have for themselves, set aside one handful of rice with every meal they prepare for their families. They give this to the church, which then sells the rice. Still running after over a hundred years, the program now raises more than a half-million dollars a year for Christian ministry throughout India.

Planned giving can be described with five Ps:

1. Priority
   "On the first day of every week, each one of you should set aside a sum of money in keeping with his income . . ." (1 Corinthians 16:2).

2. Percentage
   "This stone that I have set up as a pillar will be God's house, and of all that you give me I will give you a tenth" (Genesis 28:22).

3. Premeditated
   "Each of you should give what you have decided in your heart to give, not reluctantly or under compulsion, for God loves a cheerful giver" (2 Corinthians 9:7).

4. Progressive
   "Remember this: Whoever sows sparingly will also reap sparingly, and whoever sows generously will also reap generously" (2 Corinthians9:6).

5. Promised (based on God's promises)
   "One gives freely yet grows all the richer; another withholds what he should give, and only suffers want. Whoever brings blessing will be enriched, and one who waters will himself be watered" (Proverbs 11:24-25, ESV).

Growing in generosity involves stepping out in faith through three levels of giving.

Level 1. What we *should* give. Our first priority, based on the biblical tithe and the principle of firstfruits, is to give back a percentage of everything God gives to us. This is giving as a response to God's ownership

Level 2. What we *could* give. This takes us above the biblical minimum standard to give additional offerings. This means planning our finances so that when God gives us more, we are ready and able to give above our normal percentage. This is an expression of our desire to be a disciple, fully devoted to following Jesus and spending less on ourselves in order to serve others.

Level 3. What we *want* to give if God makes it possible. This is our heart's desire and focus to give progressively more as God rewards our faith and makes it possible.

The principle of giving God His part first

This is an extremely important principle. It is an expression of our acknowledgement that God owns everything and that everything we have belongs to him and is to be used for his purposes. Giving God his part first also breaks the power of money in our life.

The principle of the firstfruits originates in the story of Cain and Abel. Two men bring an offering to the Lord. One is of the fruit of the ground; the other, the firstborn of his flock. God accepts one and rejects the other. Why?

". . . Now Abel was a keeper of sheep, but Cain was a tiller of the ground. And in the process of time it came to pass that Cain brought an offering of the fruit of the ground to the LORD. Abel also brought of the firstborn of his flock and of their fat" (Genesis 4:2-4, NKJV).

The offering Abel brought was the firstborn of his flock, but it doesn't say that Cain brought the firstfruits of his crops. It simply says, *"Cain brought an offering of the fruit of the ground."* Cain harvested his crops and *"in the process of time"* brought his offering. It was an offering on Cain's terms. God accepted Abel's offering because it was the first of his increase. Cain's offering was rejected because it was not the first of his increase.

Giving the first of our increase to God requires faith. When a firstborn lamb is born in a flock, it's not possible to know how many more might follow, but Abel gave his firstborn lamb in faith. Cain, on the other hand, made sure he had enough for himself before giving to God. Many of us treat God as Cain did, making sure we have enough money before we see if there's anything left for God. Even if we give from what is left over, God can't accept the offering because it's not the firstfruits.

Other stories emphasise this truth. In the account of the fall of Jericho, the Lord gave strict instructions that the Israelites were not to keep any of the spoils from Jericho. The Lord declared that all of it belonged to Him. Jericho belonged to the Lord because it was the first city conquered in the Promised Land. It was firstfruits. God withheld His blessing from Israel when one man took some of the spoils for himself.

The first belongs to God. There was much more at stake than money when Abraham offered his firstborn son, Isaac. When God asked for his son, Abraham didn't wait to have ten sons before giving Isaac; he gave the first when he had only one to give. Abraham had only the promise of having more sons. It took faith for Abraham to offer Isaac, faith that God respected and blessed.

God did the same for us. He gave His first in the form of His Son, His first and only begotten Son, who was given to us while we were still sinners. God gave Jesus in faith that we might one day give our lives to Him. The gift of God's Son came before the blessing of our repentance and salvation. We give our firstfruits in much the same way. Before we see the blessing of God, we give it in faith.

Giving the firstfruits of your income says to God, "I recognize you first. I am putting You first in my life, and I trust You to take care of the rest."

More blessed to give than to receive

Before leaving Ephesus to go to Rome, Paul gave some important parting words to the elders of the church, *"And now I commend you to God and to the word of his grace . . . I coveted no one's silver or gold or apparel"* (Acts 20:31-33, ESV). Paul never asked anything *from* them, but he wanted something important *for* them. He wanted them to realize the healing power of giving and the hidden power of greed.

First, he was asking them to remember and live by the gospel, which is the word of grace. He is saying, I want you to live the gospel out. I want you to live it consistently. I want you to enjoy eternal life – the inheritance of those who believe the gospel. I did not live among you in greed and covetousness; I showed you a life poured out in deeds of mercy to the poor, as the Lord himself said, *"It is more blessed to give than to receive."*

The word used for "blessed" is *"makarios"* in Greek, meaning fullness, completeness; to be taken up into the fullness of God; to be completely healed; to experience all God wants to give us and to become all He wants us to be. The idea embodied within *"makarios"* is satisfaction from experiencing the fullness of something. The Greeks called the island of Cyprus *"e makarios"* because they considered it to be perfect, fruitful, bountiful, beautiful. *"Makarios"* is the Greek equivalent of the Hebrew *"shalom":* wholeness, healed, full, complete – everything in balance and in relationship to each other.

Experiencing the fullness of God comes through giving. We break the power of greed by giving and by experiencing God's healing power of blessing.

A student on a walk with his professor was talking about philosophy. As they went along, they saw lying in the path a pair of old shoes, which they thought must belong to a poor man who had nearly finished his day's work in a field close by.

The student turned to the professor and said, "Let's play a trick. Let's hide his shoes and then hide ourselves behind those bushes to see his reaction when he can't find them."

"My young friend," answered the professor, "we should never amuse ourselves at the expense of the poor. You could give yourself a much greater pleasure. Put a coin into each shoe, and then we'll hide ourselves and watch how the discovery affects him."

The student did so, and they both hid themselves behind the nearby bushes. The poor man soon finished his work and came across the field to the path where he had left his coat and shoes. While putting on his coat, he slipped his foot into one of his shoes. Feeling something hard, he stooped down to see what it was and found the coin. His face lit up with astonishment and wonder. He gazed at the coin, turning it over and over, looking at it again and again. He then looked around him on all sides but could see no one.

He put the money into his pocket and proceeded to put on the other shoe. His surprise was doubled on finding the other coin. His feelings overcame him, and he fell to his knees, looking up to heaven and uttering a loud and fervent thanksgiving in which he spoke of his wife, sick and helpless, and his children without bread.

The student crouched quietly in the bushes, deeply moved, his eyes filled with tears.

"Now," said the professor, "are you not much better pleased than if you had played your little trick?"

The youth replied, "You have taught me a lesson I will never forget. I feel now the truth of Jesus' words, which I never understood before. 'It is more blessed to give than to receive.'"

What a truth! It is more blessed to give than to receive. Seems counterintuitive, but it is reality. Even science has verified this through extensive psychological experiments.

In his excellent TEDx talk at Cambridge, Michael Norton makes a compelling case that spending does, indeed, buy you happiness – as long as you spend it on others!

Michael introduces the idea of social spending and explains how this increases the donor's well-being. "Spending on other people has a bigger return for you than spending on yourself."

Norton conducted experiments around the world to determine if money could buy happiness. His team approached random individuals, asked them how happy they were, and then handed them an envelope containing between five and twenty dollars. Half of the participants were asked to spend the cash on themselves; the other half, to spend it on others.

One central theme emerged from their experiments that included the likes of campus students in Canada to poor people in Uganda: those who spent money on others reported increased happiness, while those who spent it on themselves experienced no additional joy.

Norton says it does not matter how you do this. "The specific way that you spend on other people isn't nearly as important as the fact that you spend on other people."

A 2017 study said, "Generous behavior is known to increase happiness, which could thereby motivate generosity." They used functional magnetic resonance imaging (fMRI) to investigate how generosity is linked to happiness on the neural level. "The interplay of these brain regions links commitment-induced generosity with happiness."

Directional pointer #7

The seventh directional pointer in navigating the journey of a financial disciple is growing in generosity. Generosity is an outcome of financial discipleship.

CHAPTER 36

—

Compass Point Northwest: An Eternal Portfolio

You have portfolios of possessions and achievements you have accumulated over your lifetime so far. These are what you would appeal to as a basis for receiving various rewards. For example,

- a portfolio of investments will yield financial rewards,

- a portfolio of your work experiences will help you get your desired employment,

- a portfolio of your work as a student will qualify you to gain a degree, and

- a portfolio of your designs will help you get creative assignments.

An eternity portfolio, however, is far more important than the others; it will get you eternal rewards.

Why is it so important to build an eternity portfolio?

It is important because we have been designed for eternity. When we build an eternity portfolio, we are working on our destiny. *"He has made everything beautiful in its time. Also, he has put eternity into man's heart, yet so that he cannot find out what God has done from the beginning to the end"* (Ecclesiastes 3:11, ESV).

Randy Alcorn says, "All of life is a treasure hunt . . . for a perfect person in a perfect place." Our ultimate destiny is to become like Jesus – each with our unique character – and fellowship with Him forever.

Developing an eternal perspective is essential to making good decisions as a believer. We must realize that we will be called to give an account for what we have done with God's money! *"For we must all appear before the judgment seat of Christ, so that each one may receive what is due for what he has done in the body, whether good or evil"* (2 Corinthians 5:10, ESV). On the basis of this accountability, we will receive rewards. My faith in Jesus determines my eternal destination, but my behavior determines my eternal rewards.

Looking at the parable of the talents from Matthew 25, we can derive four principles about money management.

1.   We have been entrusted by God with money and possessions.

2.   We should be intentional about God's plan for investing them.

3.   We will have to give an account for our management.

4.   We will be rewarded or suffer loss based on our faithfulness or lack thereof.

Live for the line and not the dot

Randy Alcorn gives us a very useful image for building an eternal perspective. Imagine a line that goes on forever, no beginning and no end. Now draw a very small dot on the middle of this never-ending line. This dot represents our entire earthly life — almost nothing in contrast to the eternity God has in store for us. What we must do is live for the line, not for the dot.

All life on earth is like a mere breath, a soon-vanishing prelude to a never-ending life in heaven. It's the tiny dot on the line. We all live *in* the dot today, but if we are wise, we will live *for* the line. This is why we build an eternity portfolio: we want rewards that we can never outlive. This means making every decision today on the basis of its impact on eternity.

Alfred Nobel was a Swedish chemist who made a fortune by inventing dynamite and explosives for weapons. When Nobel's brother died, a newspaper accidentally printed Alfred's obituary instead. He was described as a man who became rich by enabling people to kill each other with powerful weapons. Shaken from this assessment, Nobel resolved to use his fortune to reward accomplishments that benefit humanity. We now know those rewards as the Nobel Peace Prize.

Let's put ourselves in Nobel's place. Let's read our own obituary, not as written by people, but as it would be written from heaven's point of view. Then let's use the rest of our lives to edit that obituary into what we really want it to be.

Building my eternity portfolio starts with renunciation

Renunciation is a basic requirement for flourishing in the Kingdom of heaven. Jesus' demands of the disciples were radical. *"So therefore, any one of you who does not renounce all that he has cannot be my disciple"* (Luke 14:33, ESV).

Renunciation means to place everything at God's disposal. It is giving up every single one of our own dreams and desires, yielding these to the overarching eternal plans of God.

"Sell your possessions and give to the needy. Provide yourselves with moneybags that do not grow old, with a treasure in the heavens that does not fail, where no thief approaches and no moth destroys" (Luke 12:33, ESV).

Rewards are promised as a result of renunciation – not only now but also in the age to come. *"And he said to them, 'Truly, I say to you, there is no one who has left house or wife or brothers or parents or children, for the sake of the kingdom of God, who will not receive many times more in this time, and in the age to come eternal life'"* (Luke 18:29-30, ESV).

John Wesley

John Wesley knew grinding poverty as a child. His father, Samuel Wesley, was the Anglican priest in one of England's lowest-paying parishes.

It probably came as a surprise to John Wesley that although God had called him to follow his father's vocation, he had not also called him to be poor like his father. Instead of being a parish priest, John felt God's direction to teach at Oxford University. There he was elected a fellow of Lincoln College, and his financial status changed dramatically. His position usually paid him at least thirty pounds a year: more than enough for a single man to live on. John seems to have enjoyed his relative prosperity. He spent his money on playing cards, tobacco, and brandy.

While at Oxford, an incident changed his perspective on money. He had just finished paying for some pictures for his room when one of the chambermaids came to his door. It was a cold winter day, and he noticed that she had nothing to protect her except a thin linen gown. He reached into his pocket to give her some money to buy a coat but found he had too little left. Immediately the thought struck him that the Lord was not pleased with the way he had spent his money.

He asked himself, "Will thy Master say, 'Well done, good and faithful steward'? Thou hast adorned thy walls with the money which might have screened this poor creature from the cold! O justice! O mercy! Are not these pictures the blood of this poor maid?"

Perhaps as a result of this incident in 1731, Wesley began to limit his expenses so that he would have more money to give to the poor. He records that one year his income was 30 pounds and his living expenses 28 pounds, so he had 2 pounds to give away. The next year his income doubled, but he still managed to live on 28 pounds, so he had 32 pounds to give to the poor. In the third year, his income jumped to 90 pounds. Instead of letting his expenses rise with his income, he kept them to 28 pounds and gave away 62 pounds. In the fourth year, he received 120 pounds. As before, his expenses were 28 pounds, so his giving rose to 92 pounds.

Wesley felt that the Christian should not merely tithe but give away all extra income once the family and creditors were taken care of. He believed that with increasing income, what should rise is not the Christian's standard of living but the standard of giving.

His lifestyle was measured by his statement, "I value all things by the price they shall gain in eternity."

The financial disciple will invest his or her time, talents, and treasure to help others learn to follow Christ, teaching them to obey all he has commanded us to do.

Welcoming people to eternity

Some lines from a poem have stuck in my memory many years now.

> When the voice of the Master is calling
> And the gates of heaven unfold,
> And the saints of all ages are gathering
> And are thronging the city of gold;
> How my heart shall o'erflow with rapture
> If a brother shall greet me and say,
> "You pointed my footsteps to heaven,
> You told me of Jesus, the Way."

Jesus gave a one-sentence explanation of the parable of the so-called "Unrighteous Steward" – a parable we find really difficult to understand. I am thankful that his explanation was clear. *"And I tell you, make friends for yourselves by means of unrighteous wealth, so that when it fails they may receive you into the eternal dwellings"* (Luke 16:9, ESV).

Jesus is saying that we are to use money, which is inherently unrighteous, to develop relationships with people so that they may experience eternity.

For the financial disciple, this means that the most important goal is not to make money but to make friends and influence people for the Lord. As I look back on life, nothing has given me more joy or satisfaction than hearing from people, "Thank you so much for showing me how I can follow Jesus." I thank God that this happens regularly. This is the reason I can renounce pleasures of the world. This is the reason I can live with less than my friends and neighbors have.

I have known many businesspeople who have been very successful. I like to ask them, "When you look back on your career, what do you regret the most?" In nearly every case, I hear the answer, "I wish I would have spent more time developing relationships with family and friends." No one has said, "I wish I would have spent more time working." All too often, meaningful relationships have been sacrificed on the altar of success.

Building the financial disciple's eternity portfolio focuses on spending their money for the good news of the Kingdom and winning souls for Christ. May our heavenly Father teach us how we can invest in people so that they may know eternal life and be welcomed into *"the eternal dwellings."* The original Greek word for dwellings is *"skene,"* which means a "tent." In Scripture, our bodies are called tents. You, your real personality, now dwells in an earthly tent, but when you go beyond death, you will find another tent, also with form and shape. This will be an eternal tent, an everlasting body that will be perfect for those accepted and welcomed by Christ.

All that God gives us is a sacred trust in view of eternity. In our everyday lives, we must deal with everything entrusted to us in the light of its impact on people's eternity. The financial disciple will ask, "What can I do with this money to help people experience eternity?" instead of asking, "What can I buy with this money to make my life more pleasurable?"

I was privileged to know an Indonesian businessman, owner of a huge insurance company with over seven thousand employees. Each morning before work, he would lie face down on the floor in his office to pray. "Each day I want to be ready for eternity," he would say. "Each day I want to count for eternity." Many people in that company found Jesus.

Introducing people to grace

Salvation, of course, can never be bought with money — it is a free gift of God, an act of grace.

Jesus is asking us to penetrate the world of money with grace, being faithful to God as our only master.

A wonderful picture of grace is Victor Hugo's story *Les Misérables.* Valjean is an ex-convict on parole, embittered by the discrimination he receives everywhere he goes because of his criminal status. He has just been taken in by a bishop for the night after being kicked out of everywhere else he had found to stay.

In response to the mercy shown to him, however, Valjean robs the bishop's house and runs away with silverware in the night. Soon caught by the police, he lies that the bishop had made a present of the silver. Not believing him, the police bring him back to the bishop's house to test the story, expecting to arrest Valjean.

The bishop, however, instead of taking his silver back and condemning Valjean, tells the officers that he had indeed given the silver to Valjean. Not only that, he offers some additional candlesticks that he says Valjean must have forgotten in his haste. This is a graphic example of turning the other cheek after being slapped in the face, of giving his cloak when asked for his shirt – all because of his zeal to redeem Valjean.

The bishop draws near to Valjean and says, "Jean Valjean, my brother, you no longer belong to evil, but to good. It is your soul that I buy from you; I withdraw it from black thoughts and the spirit of perdition, and I give it to God."

Valjean, unable to comprehend this radical act of grace, renounces his old life and follows the bishop's command to "use this precious silver to become an honest man."

Valjean was redeemed by grace and entered a new reality. This is the purpose of using money in a way that doesn't make earthly economic sense: to introduce people into God's world of grace. Is it possible to "buy back" someone's soul through acts of selfless kindness? That is exactly what Jesus did for you and me.

Next steps

In whom could you invest? Who is God bringing alongside you to disciple?

I have been able to find people in over 45 nations in whom I can invest time, resources, training, and equipping so that they, in turn, can disciple people in their own cities and nations. I should say, rather, that God has found them for me.

My guiding principle has been the prayer of Jesus for His disciples, *"I have revealed you to those whom you gave me out of the world. They were yours; you gave them to me and they have obeyed your word. Now they know that everything you have given me comes from you. For I gave them the words you gave me and they accepted them. They knew with certainty that I came from you, and they believed that you sent me"* (John 17:6-8).

Our task is to reveal Jesus to those whom God gives us *"out of the world."* In your everyday work, God will be pointing you to people with whom you will have some kind of connection, with whom you can start a relationship. He or she will be someone who responds in some way to your life and mission. Watch for people like this in the expectation that God is giving them to you. Your task, then, is to follow Jesus' example and give them the words the Father gives you.

This begins, of course, with prayer: "Lord, please reveal to me the person or persons I could help know you better, to obey your call and accept your teaching."

I find it a fascinating contrast that when Jesus prayed before raising Lazarus from the dead, He prayed very quickly, for just a moment. Before appointing His twelve disciples, however, he prayed all night! *"One of those days Jesus went out to a mountainside to pray, and spent the night praying to God. When morning came, he called his disciples to him and chose twelve of them, whom he also designated apostles"* (Luke 6:12-13).

In His prayer for the disciples, Jesus prayed, *"I pray for them. I am not praying for the world, but for those you have given me, for they are yours"* (John 17:9). Of course Jesus had a burden for the world, but He was praying here for *"those you have given me."* The Father will give you people if you ask and stay alert for His answer.

The Lord has given me several promises during my disciple-making ministry, all of which He has kept.

I wanted my life to be significant and count for eternity. My prayer was that many would come to Christ and be discipled. He promised, *"The least of you will become a thousand, the smallest a mighty nation. I am the Lord; in its time I will do this swiftly"* (Isaiah 60:22).

Looking back on more than forty organizations I have helped pioneer, many thousands have been discipled.

This comes by giving my life, which is always a struggle. *"If you spend yourselves in behalf of the hungry . . . your people will rebuild the ancient ruins and will raise up the foundation of many generations . . ."* (Isaiah 58:10-12).

Barnabas was dedicated to the mission of Jesus. We read that he sold some real estate and brought the proceeds to the apostles in Jerusalem to help the early church grow (Acts 4:37). When Paul visited Jerusalem after his conversion, the apostles could not believe that the same Paul who had persecuted the church could be a disciple! He needed someone to help.

Along came Barnabas, whose name means "son of encouragement." Acts 11 records Barnabas fetching Paul from Tarsus and bringing him to Antioch in 45 AD. Barnabas and Paul traveled together in 46 AD. They traveled throughout Cyprus and Cilicia on the first missionary journey – working together on a common trade and recruiting disciples for the new churches (Acts 13).

Barnabas recruited Paul to help him teach the new followers of Christ in Antioch (Acts 11:25-26). Barnabas guided Paul during his development from a novice follower of Christ to the greatest propagator of the faith in the early church. Later, Barnabas took on Mark as a disciple when Paul refused to continue working with Mark (Acts 15:38-39).

Paul carried on Barnabas's example by training Timothy. Paul then wrote to Timothy, *"what you have heard from me in the presence of many witnesses entrust to faithful men, who will be able to teach others also"* (2 Timothy 2:2, ESV). Here we see four generations of disciples: Paul — Timothy — faithful men — others.

My prayer for you is that you will raise up the foundation of many generations of disciples. Paul wrote that we can give our lives to build a foundation made from *"gold, silver, precious stones,"* or from *"wood, hay, straw"* (1 Corinthians 3:12, ESV). In other words, we can give our lives for that which will last for eternity or for those things that will soon be consumed.

People are precious in God's eyes; they will last for eternity. Giving my life for people will yield eternal significance.

> *"Since you are precious and honored in my sight,*
> *and because I love you,*
> *I will give people in exchange for you,*
> *nations in exchange for your life"* (Isaiah 43:4).

May He give you faithful, available, and teachable people with whom you can walk and impart what Jesus has taught you. May your people impact many nations for the Kingdom!

—

FINISHING WELL

—

Howard Dayton is the founder of Compass – finances God's way.
He has written some closing thoughts on financial discipleship and
finishing well.

When people used to ask evangelist Billy Graham how they could pray for him, he invariably responded, "Pray that I finish my life well and don't dishonor the Lord." He recognized how rare it was for people to remain faithful to the Lord, fully engaged in their calling to the end.

Can you imagine anything better than finishing well and having these words of Jesus ring in your ears throughout all eternity? *"Well done, good and faithful servant . . . enter into the joy of your master"* (Matthew 25:21, ESV).

It sounds wonderful, but it can be a challenge. Of the 2,930 people mentioned in the Bible, we know significant details of only one hundred. And of those one hundred, only about one-third finished well. Most of the other two-thirds failed in the second half of their lives.

Solomon is a classic example of someone who started out great but failed miserably later in life. Think about it: few people have started out as well and with more promise than Solomon.

- He was loved by God. *". . . The Lord loved [Solomon] and sent word through Nathan the prophet that they should name him Jedidiah (which means beloved of the Lord)"* (2 Samuel 12:24-25, NLT).
- His father was King David, who authored most of the of Psalms and was described by God as *"a man after my own heart"* (Acts 13:22)
- Solomon made great choices early and was given more wisdom than any person. He wrote most of the book of Proverbs.

But then Solomon stopped following the Lord and descended into a life of disobedience. Deuteronomy 17 lists three things the kings of Israel were prohibited from doing.

- The king must not acquire great numbers of horses for himself or make the people return to Egypt to get more of them.
- He must not accumulate large amounts of silver and gold.

- He must not take many wives, or his heart will be led astray.

So, what does Solomon do?

- He acquires twelve thousand horses imported from Egypt.
- He amasses silver and gold for himself.
- He has seven hundred wives, and his wives lead him astray.

He was completely disobedient to the Lord. And the consequences were disastrous for Solomon, his family, and for the entire nation of Israel. Clearly, starting well does not guarantee that a person will finish well.

In your journey with the Lord, it's not how you start that matters. It's how you finish. The Christian life isn't a hundred-meter dash; it's a marathon. Long races don't require speed; they require determination and finishing power — fixing our eyes on the prize and finishing well.

Paul illustrates this from his own experience. *". . . one thing I do: forgetting what lies behind and reaching forward to what lies ahead, I press on toward the goal for the prize of the upward call of God in Christ Jesus"* (Philippians 3:13-14, NASB).

Finishing well doesn't mean finishing with a perfect record. But it does mean learning from our mistakes, getting back on course, and pursuing the Lord with our whole heart. We need to work hard at building the kingdom of God as long as we are able — regardless of past failures. In the many years of Compass, we've seen people really struggle to finish well, and we've seen people flourish. We've noticed that the strong finishers have several key characteristics in common.

Bible-Based

"All Scripture is God-breathed and is useful for teaching, rebuking, correcting and training in righteousness, so that the man of God may be thoroughly equipped for every good work" (2 Timothy 3:16-17). Let's take a closer look at how Scripture has the ability to fully equip us on our Finishing Well journey.

There is simply no healthy Christian life apart from God's word. In the Bible, God tells us about Himself, enabling us to learn His ways and will. Only in the Scriptures do we find how to live in a way that truly pleases God.

When Jesus asked people about their understanding of the Scriptures, He often began with the words, "Have you not read?" He assumed that those claiming to be the people of God would have read the word of God. Unfortunately, this just isn't the case. A survey found that only 18 percent of Christians read the Bible every day, and 23 percent never do. So let's look at some ways we can break these trends and consistently be in God's word.

First, find the time. Perhaps one of the main reasons Christians never read through the entire Bible is its sheer length — it's BIG! At first glance it can feel overwhelming. But do you realize that you can read the entire Bible in 71 hours? Audio recordings prove it. In no more than 15 minutes a day you can read through the Bible in a year's time.

Another great practice is to find a Bible-reading plan. It's no wonder that those who simply open the Bible randomly each day soon drop the practice. Fortunately, there are some great Bible-reading plans available to help you stay consistent. Some Bibles are designed specifically to guide you through completing them in a year.

Each time you read, look for one phrase or verse to meditate on. Take a few minutes to think deeply about it. This will change your life. The Lord commanded Joshua, *"This book of the law shall not depart from your mouth, but you shall meditate on it day and night, so that you may be careful to do according to all that is written in it; for then . . . you will have success"* (Joshua 1:8, NASB).

Now, you may be thinking, "That's great for Joshua, but I've got a business or a household to run! I can't think about the Bible all day long. I've got decisions to make. It just isn't practical."

Let me assure you that meditation is the most practical thing in the world. Joshua didn't just sit around all day thinking about the Scriptures. He had two million people to manage. He was as busy, if not busier, than you are. So how does a busy person meditate on the Bible? Simple – read through a portion, and when a verse is especially meaningful to you, write it down. Take it with you, review it, and think about it during the day.

Finally, find a Bible study. Most of us will be way more consistent if we become involved in a Bible study. We need the encouragement and accountability of a group. And one of the greatest benefits of a group is developing close relationships with others who are also seeking to know the Lord better.

Christ-Centered

God's word is incredibly important in helping people finish well, but so is being Christ-centered. Since this may not be a term you hear every day, let's dig a little deeper into what it really means. It's actually pretty simple: if Jesus is the Lord of your life, you're going to do what He tells you to do. That's what it means to be Christ-centered.

When people surrender to the Lordship of Jesus Christ, they are acknowledging God's ownership and giving up their personal rights. This kind of obedience is a common theme we see among those who finish well. So, let's explore what it takes to be Christ-centered.

Our desire at Compass is threefold: helping people experience financial faithfulness, drawing them closer to the Lord, and encouraging them to surrender themselves to God. This includes recognizing that God owns it all, just as Psalm 24:1 tells us: *"The earth is the Lord's and everything in it."*

Being Christ-centered isn't something we do just once; it is something we should strive to do every day, hour, and minute of our lives. It's a constant in the lives of those who finish well, and although it sounds challenging, there are several things we can do to make it a constant in our finishing-well journey.

A key factor in being Christ-centered is allowing the Lord to direct our paths. God is the only one who knows the direction we should take in our lives. Just as Israel was guided in the wilderness by the cloud and fire, and the apostles responded to Jesus when He said, *"Follow me,"* we must constantly be sensitive to the direction of the Lord in our business, our relationships, our ministry, and our daily lives. And this applies not only to the big decisions we face but also our small everyday decisions as well.

Paul gives us a good example of being Christ-centered. *"For I resolved to know nothing while I was with you except Jesus Christ and him crucified. I came to you in weakness and fear, and with much trembling. My message and my preaching were not with wise and persuasive words, but with a demonstration of the Spirit's power, so that your faith might not rest on men's wisdom, but on God's power"* (1 Corinthians 2:2-5).

There is a lot of noise in this world on how to make the best decisions, how to be successful, and how to be the best you. Christ-centered people cover their ears to drown out this noise. They don't trust in the clever things of the world, but rather, humbly depend upon Jesus Christ to guide and direct their steps.

A second important factor in being Christ-centered is fruitfulness. A Christ-centered person recognizes that the fruitfulness of their lives is a direct result of their relationship with the Lord. John 15:1-5 tells us, *"I am the true vine, and my Father is the gardener . . . No branch can bear fruit by itself; it must remain in the vine. Neither can you bear fruit unless you remain in me. I am the vine; you are the branches. If a man remains in me and I in him, he will bear much fruit; apart from me you can do nothing."* The more obedient and dependent we are on the Lord, the more fruitful we will be in our ability to love and serve others.

Prayer-Driven

James 1:5 tells us, *"If any of you lacks wisdom, you should ask God, who gives generously to all without finding fault, and it will be given to you."* Seeking the Lord's direction, provision, and protection through prayer must be a constant focus for us on our journey to finishing well. Prayer makes us more like Jesus as it shows us God's heart and reveals His wisdom. It is essential to us in understanding and doing His will.

If prayer could have been unnecessary for anyone, surely it would have been Jesus, the sinless Son of God. However, it was one of the dominant habits of His life and a frequent theme in His teaching.

> Mark 1:35 tells us that *"Very early in the morning, while it was still dark, Jesus got up, left the house and went off to a solitary place, where he prayed."*

> Luke 6:12-13 tells us that *"Jesus went out to a mountainside to pray, and spent the night praying to God. When morning came, he called his disciples to him and chose twelve of them, whom he also designated apostles."*

> And Luke 5:16 tells us, *"But Jesus often withdrew to lonely places and prayed."* This isn't something he did on occasion but was something that was a normal part of his life.

Sometimes Jesus got up early in the morning to pray, sometimes he spent the whole night praying, and sometimes he would just go off to a quiet place and pray. Regardless of when or where he prayed, it is clear that even in the demands of His public ministry, Jesus consistently spent time alone with His Heavenly Father.

Throughout the history of the church, those serving in leadership have recognized the importance of prayer. Samuel Chadwick said, "The one concern of the devil is to keep Christians from praying. He fears nothing from our prayerless work, prayerless religion. He laughs at our toil, he mocks our wisdom, but he trembles when we pray."

One of the most important factors in true intimacy with the Lord is honesty in our prayer lives. As C. S. Lewis said, we should "lay before Him what is in us, not what ought to be in us." The Lord is thrilled that you are willing to come to Him as His child and spend time with Him, so come as naturally as you can. If you are hurting, share your pain. If you are confused, seek His guidance. If your joy is bubbling over, let it bubble over in praise. Being honest and transparent in your prayer time can take your prayer life *and* your relationship with the Lord to another level.

Holy Spirit-Led

We cannot be truly Christ-centered, Bible-based, or Prayer-driven without being led by the Holy Spirit. Just as Jesus depended on the Holy Spirit to reveal the will of the Father to Him, we need to be completely dependent on Him to reveal God's will to us.

John 14:15-17 tells us, *"If you love me, keep my commands. And I will ask the Father, and he will give you another advocate to help you and be with you forever – the Spirit of truth. The world cannot accept him, because it neither sees him nor knows him. But you know him, for he lives with you and will be in you."*

When we translate the Greek word for advocate, we see that it refers to someone coming alongside somebody, someone who plays the role of an encourager and urges people on. Our advocate isn't just some random spirit floating around; the Holy Spirit has a home, and that home is you. He literally lives in those who love the Lord – every believer.

Of all the gifts given to us, none is greater than the presence of the Holy Spirit. So, let's take a closer look at some of the ways the Holy Spirit helps us on our journey of finishing well.

One of the many ways that the Holy Spirit helps us is through insight. Think of it this way: have you ever had a verse you had read years earlier suddenly came to mind – exactly when you needed it most?

That's not luck, and it's not a coincidence. It's the Holy Spirit prompting you with God's provision for that moment.

John 14:26 tells us, "But the Helper, the Holy Spirit, whom the Father will send in My name, He will teach you all things, and bring to your remembrance all that I said to you" (NASB).

In addition to insight from the past, the Holy Spirit gives us insight into the present. As we are reading and studying Scripture, it is the Holy Spirit who teaches us, guides us, and helps us to understand the truth of God's word.

The Holy Spirit also teaches us to be more like Jesus. *"And we all, who with unveiled faces contemplate the Lord's glory, are being transformed into his image with ever-increasing glory, which comes from the Lord, who is the Spirit" (2 Corinthians 3:18).*

Although Moses got to experience God's glory on a mountaintop, the Holy Spirit gives us the opportunity to experience God's glory each and every day, no matter where we are!

Theologian Warren Wiersbe says it this way, "Moses reflected the glory of God, but you and I may radiate the glory of God. When we meditate on God's word and in it see God's Son, then the Spirit transforms us! We become more like the Lord Jesus Christ as we grow from glory to glory."

It is the Holy Spirit that equips us to be more like Christ, constantly transforming us and renewing us into His image.

And the Holy Spirit is also the giver of gifts – gifts given to believers that are essential to the proper functioning of the Church. No one receives all the gifts; they're uniquely dispensed to God's people according to His plan for each person.

"Now there are varieties of gifts, but the same Spirit; and there are varieties of service, but the same Lord; and there are varieties of activities, but it is the same God who empowers them all in everyone.

To each is given the manifestation of the Spirit for the common good" (1 Corinthians 12:4-8, ESV).

These gifts are given to us to equip us for the calling God has put on our lives. They aren't meant to be put on the shelf for a later date; they are given to us for the here and now, and for a purpose. So, I'd encourage you to think about how God is calling you and how you are using the gifts the Spirit has given you – for His glory.

Discipleship-Focused

Matthew 28:19-20 tells us, "Therefore go and make disciples of all nations, baptizing them in the name of the Father and of the Son and of the Holy Spirit, and teaching them to obey everything I have commanded you. And surely I am with you always, to the very end of the age."

The word "disciple" essentially means "learner." The Great Commission, the last instruction Jesus gave, reflects His personal priority and greatest investment of time: making disciples by teaching them how to obey everything He commanded.

Although Jesus taught the multitudes, He focused on the few. Jesus knew that making disciples was crucial for succeeding generations to follow. The same Holy Spirit gives each member of the body different gifts, but all of us are commanded to make disciples.

A big part of the Finishing Well journey is being discipleship-focused. This means examining how we are personally growing as disciples and also how we are making disciples by pouring our lives into others. So, let's explore some ways we can be discipleship-focused.

One of the main characteristics of disciples is that they strive to imitate Jesus. Luke 6:40 tells us that *"A disciple is not above his teacher, but everyone when he is fully trained will be like his teacher"* (ESV).

When it comes to discipleship, the goal is to imitate the life of Christ. And in order to help believers grow as disciples, we must be willing not only to *tell* them how but also to *show* them how. Paul said, *"Be imitators of me, as I am of Christ"* (1 Corinthians 11:1, ESV). And in Philippians 4:9 he wrote, *"What you have learned and received and heard and seen in me – practice these things, and the God of peace will be with you"* (ESV). He not only gave verbal instructions to the believers, he also lived out his faith before them.

Another key characteristic of disciples is that they bear fruit. Let's look at what Jesus says in John 15:5. *"I am the vine; you are the branches. Whoever abides in me and I in him, he it is that bears much fruit, for apart from me you can do nothing"* (ESV).

As we grow in our discipleship journey, we should start producing fruit, the fruit of the Spirit: love, joy, peace, patience, kindness, goodness, faithfulness, gentleness, and self-control. This doesn't mean we have to be perfect in all of these areas, but it does mean that the fruit of the Spirit will become more apparent in our lives as we grow on our discipleship journey.

Multiplication is the goal when it comes to discipleship. Disciples make other disciples: they replicate themselves; they reproduce. They desire to see lives transformed and see people grow in their relationship with the Lord.

Jesus focused on growing His disciples, but He had a greater end in mind: He wanted them to reproduce themselves. In the Great Commission, Jesus passes the baton to them, telling them to go and make disciples of all the nations.

Disciples aren't supposed to just sit on what they've learned: they are commanded to share the gospel with others and teach believers to be imitators of Christ. Disciples go after people with God's love, sharing Jesus with them. They also pursue other believers, mentoring and encouraging them in their faith. Inevitably, a person who is finishing well is someone who is walking alongside others on their discipleship journey.

Closing

Thank you for spending this time with us. In closing, I'd like to leave you with a few thoughts that have been powerful motivators for me.

Nothing on this planet comes close to knowing Jesus Christ and living a life that pleases Him.

> Leave your mistakes behind.
> Be courageous.
> Stay focused on Christ.
> Never give up.

Jesus finished well when He said, *"I have brought you glory on earth by finishing the work you gave me to do"* (John 17:4, ESV).

Paul finished well when he said, *"I have fought the good fight, I have finished the course, I have kept the faith"* (2 Timothy 4:7, NASB).

Our prayer is that you will finish well, too. That you will complete the task the Lord has given you so that you will hear these words ring in your ears throughout eternity: *"Well done, good and faithful servant . . . enter into the joy of your master"* (Matthew 25:21, ESV).

Howard Dayton

Howard Dayton, Founder, Compass – finances God's Way

Continue The Journey...

Congratulations on completing *Financial Discipleship... investing in eternity.* We hope the Lord has had a significant impact on your financial discipleship journey through this book.

The financial discipleship journey is one that doesn't end until we hear the words *"well done, good and faithful servant."* We encourage you to continue on this journey in one of two ways.

Continue your journey by engaging in studies, tools, and resources that will help you grow. Visit us at **ContinueGrowing.org** to learn more.

Continue your journey by paying it forward and helping others grow. To learn more, visit us at **HelpOthersGrow.org**.

Thank you for the time and effort you have invested in this book. We pray the Lord will draw you ever nearer to Him as you continue to grow and help others grow.